The author
Jeanne Holloway is Senior Learning Support Adviser at Esl[...]
is also a freelance author and FE consultant. Jeanne has sp[...]
encouraging students of all ages to 'learn how to learn' through her many
publications and contributions to teacher training.

**The author and publishers would like to acknowledge the collaboration
of Esher College in the production of this book.**

Layout: Charlotte Chard
Cover art: Tony Ashton

Any advice given on answering exam questions is the sole responsibility of the author and
has not been approved or provided by any exam board.

The publishers grant permission for multiple copies of any material from this book to be
made within the place of purchase for use solely within that institution.

ISBN 0 9520683 6 2
British Library Cataloguing in Publication Data. A catalogue record of this book is
available from the British Library.

Published 1999, reprinted 2001, 2003

Cooksbridge House, Cooksbridge, Lewes, East Sussex BN8 4SR
Tel and fax (01273) 401714
E mail: connect.pub@mistral.co.uk

THE LEARNING KIT
Contents

Section 1
IMPROVING YOUR LEARNING
Teachers' notes
1.1 Getting to know your brain
1.3 Memory
1.4 Memaids
1.5 What sort of student is this?
1.6 Study skills audit
1.7 Learning styles
1.8 Brainstorming
1.10 Thinking about thinking: problem solving
1.12 Solving study problems
1.15 Time management
1.17 Short term timetable
1.18 Using teachers' comments

Section 2
WORKING WITH OTHERS
Teachers' notes
2.1 Similarities and differences
2.3 Listening to others
2.5 Analysing groups
2.7 Roles in groups
2.8 Body language in groups
2.10 Group dynamics
2.11 Group work evaluation

Section 3
READING
Teachers' notes
3.1 Preparing to read
3.3 Reading with a sense of purpose (1)
3.4 Reading with a sense of purpose (2)
3.5 Changing words to pictures
3.7 SQ3R
3.9 Skimming, rapid reading and scanning

Section 4
NOTE MAKING AND NOTE TAKING
Teachers' notes
4.1 Linear notes
4.2 Visual notes
4.4 Using key words
4.5 Taking notes from a lecture
4.7 Mind-mapping
4.8 Storyboarding
4.10 Summarising

Section 5
MAKING PRESENTATIONS
Teachers' notes
5.1 What makes a good presentation?
5.2 Planning a presentation
5.5 Preparing what to say
5.8 Using body language
5.10 Using visual aids

Section 6
WRITING AT LENGTH: ESSAYS, SPELLING AND PUNCTUATION
Teachers' notes
6.1 Decoding essay titles
6.3 Planning essays
6.5 Paragraphs
6.7 Connecting phrases and sentences
6.8 Introductions and conclusions
6.10 Spell well
6.13 Improving punctuation

Section 7
DEALING WITH STRESS
Teachers' notes
7.1 Recognising and dealing with stress
7.4 Stress and time management
7.5 Exams and stress

Section 8
PREPARING FOR EXAMS
Teachers' notes
8.1 Organising revision
8.3 Planning a revision timetable
8.5 Making revision cards
8.6 Quick revision
8.7 Key words in exams
8.9 Understanding exams
8.11 What sort of exam taker are you?

© **CONNECT** Publications 1999

Section 1

IMPROVING YOUR LEARNING

Teachers' notes
- 1.1 Getting to know your brain
- 1.3 Memory
- 1.4 Memaids
- 1.5 What sort of student is this?
- 1.6 Study skills audit
- 1.7 Learning styles
- 1.8 Brainstorming
- 1.10 Thinking about thinking: problem solving
- 1.12 Solving study problems
- 1.15 Time management
- 1.17 Short term timetable
- 1.18 Using teachers' comments

Teachers' notes
IMPROVING YOUR LEARNING

This section aims to provoke thinking about learning. The activities encourage students to discuss and evaluate their study needs.

The **Getting to know your brain** activity can lead to fruitful discussion of the importance of using left and right brain techniques in combination to maximise learning potential. For example, why do most of us learn songs and jingles with ease yet not facts? Why do we prefer colourful posters to pages of text? A useful extension activity is to ask students to make a poster or tape or devise a jingle for an aspect of their studies they experience difficulty with. Ask them to write a sentence or two explaining why this would help the information go into long term memory.

The **Memory** activities encourage the use of *memaids* – any catchy way of remembering for the long term. Extend this activity by asking students how they would use 'memaids' to teach a younger child, say, the days of the week, the months of the year or some famous dates. For example, *'in 1666 the town of London burnt to sticks'*. Thinking about how they would teach someone else in a way that they will remember in the long term will help students to understand how 'left brain learning' can easily be adapted to 'right brain thinking.'

What sort of student is this? encourages students to look objectively at study related needs as they take on the role of adviser. This activity can usefully be extended by asking students to write just two headings - *Strengths* and *Weaknesses* - and to fill this in appropriately with the scores of 1 and 2 being placed under *Weaknesses* and Scores of 4 and 5 under *Strengths*. Discuss the 'average' score of 3 separately, focusing on what could be done to move these scores up to the *Strengths* area.

The **Study skills audit** activity can be extended by talking about SMART targets. To be SMART targets must be Specific, Measurable, Achievable, Relevant to needs and Time bonded. Students can gain a great deal of self confidence from making SMART targets as they are realistic rather then idealistic.

Learning styles. Students can apply the idea of '*learning styles*' to a wide range of problems. Another example is, *'I am hungry and there is no food in the house. I have no money'*.

The *Active* approach person may decide to see what is growing in the garden or look at what houseplants are edible. The *Practical* person may think about the many thousands of people in the world who are also hungry and find out how long s/he can go without food before it becomes detrimental to health. The *Thinker* may brainstorm the possibilities and choices available to relieve the hunger and might make a flow chart along the following lines: *Am I hungry? – Yes. Why am I hungry? What is hunger?* and so on.

The idea is to encourage careful consideration of the *approach* they would take to the situation rather than always going in 'feet first' in search of an immediate answer. Students could then discuss how they might approach a study-related situation such as *'I have an exam in two weeks time'*, *'I have missed a lot of coursework'* or *'I need A's but I keep getting D's'*.

The focus of the **Brainstorming** activity is to enable students to understand that brainstorming is *not* about making neat lists and diagrams - it is about *pouring out* thoughts – both appropriate and inappropriate – for a given time. Time on task is very important as, otherwise, thoughts wander. Suggested warm up or follow up activities could be to ask students to write non stop for one minute any ideas that come to mind from stimulus words such as *shells*, *webs*, or *towers*. For example a one minute student brainstorm on *'Shells'* might yield: *petrol, derelict houses, sand, sea, bombshells, meringues, earrings, ears, tortoises, crab shells, funfairs, the shell of an idea, childhood, war, science, fossils*.

Thinking about thinking: problem solving aims to encourage the breaking down of study related problems into manageable proportions by raising questions. Students should *not* be asked to come up with answers. As a warm up or conclusion activity students might benefit from formulating ten questions that they might raise if, for example, they went out one Saturday and found that the streets were empty and the shops closed, or they turned on the television to find the word *'Alert'* was displayed on the screen of every television channel. They could then transfer their question raising techniques to a study related task such as *'I have been given a list of essential further reading texts that must be completed by next week'*. Questions raised might take the form of *'Where do I get the books?' 'What if the library doesn't have them?' 'How do I plan my time?' 'When do I read them?' 'Do I need to make notes?'* and so on.

Solving study problems is about thinking ahead by identifying potential problems. For example students often think they will get a book from the library and read it that evening without thinking about the possibility that the book may not be available. Discuss what potential problems can be identified in the following tasks: *Working with a group in order to make a video. Videoing a programme essential to study. Copying hand written notes onto the word processor in one afternoon. Photocopying a friend's notes for your own revision. Taking an exam.*

Time management. Working backwards from deadlines is an important part of thinking about time management. A blank **Short term timetable** is provided to assist this process. To help students' management of time when undertaking extended project work they could be asked to think about the advantages of checking and improving work and the length of time needed to write the final draft, bibliography and references.

The purpose of the **Using teachers' comments** activity is to encourage consideration of the criteria used for allocating marks, how to use marking comments and what to change in order to improve marks. Students can discuss the different assessment criteria in each of their subjects. A useful extension activity is to write marking comments for an ideal / top marks essay /assignment with comments relating to both content and presentation.

GETTING TO KNOW YOUR BRAIN

Have you ever thought seriously how you learn? Maybe you're so intent on learning *about* a particular subject that you haven't considered *how* to learn about it. This can make a big difference. Think about how you learnt to walk and talk. Do you ever wake up and think, *'Oh dear, I've forgotten how to walk so I won't go out today'*? You don't because you have learnt the skill, retained it and practise it regularly.

How did you learn the following skills? Tick each relevant box.

	By hearing	By seeing	By doing	By practising	By reading
Talking					
Singing					
Reading					
Riding a bike					
Swimming					
Word processing					
Climbing					
Writing					
Counting					
Drawing					

You can probably see from the above table that you have learnt a lot by **doing** and **practising**. That is, through practical activities. How can you make your own study more practical? Maybe, if you are studying English, you could read a play aloud or record some parts. Or transfer ordinary written notes to a drawing or chart when revising.

It's difficult to study effectively without being aware of how the brain actually works. It is divided into two hemispheres, the left and the right.

Left hemisphere	**Right hemisphere**
good at	*good at*
words	guessing
numbers	arts subjects
maths	imagining
analysis	colours
science	drawing
dealing with time	designing
thinking logically	identifying alternatives
being practical	music
	thinking in pictures

IMPROVING YOUR LEARNING

In order to maximise your potential for learning you need to use the strengths of both hemispheres to the full.

Here is a piece of text. It has no illustrations and is definitely 'left hemisphere biased'. Read it and then introduce some 'right hemisphere' thinking from the list in order to help remember it.

> It is an evening in autumn. Pegeen Milke is seated at a table in the public house drawing up an order for her trousseau and other requisites for her forthcoming wedding. As she writes her fiancé, Shawn Keogh, looks in apprehensively and asks Pegeen where her father is. Shawn, a very reserved, cautious young man tells Pegeen that he deliberated for some time before taking the liberty of dropping in to see her on his way by the tavern.
>
> Pegeen informs Shawn that her father, Michael James Flaherty, has gone to fetch Philly Cullen. They and several others are about to set out for Kate Cassidy's wake. Shawn, timid as ever, is surprised to learn that Pegeen's father is going so far at such a late hour. Pegeen complains that she has been left alone to fend for herself and Shawn assures her that when they are married he will keep her company.

1. Draw or make a diagram in colour to depict the text.
2. Write an alternative version of the story.
3. Write a jingle, poem or song which tells the story in the text.
4. Highlight significant points in the text.

Which right brain hemisphere 'techniques' did you use in completing these tasks?

You will find that you will remember the text details for longer if you have used your brain effectively.

Now look back at the brain hemispheres and learn them using some of the techniques above.

Left hemisphere	Right hemisphere

IMPROVING YOUR LEARNING

MEMORY

Have you ever despaired of your memory? Have you worried that it will let you down in the exams? Maybe you've sometimes thought it has completely abandoned you. Don't worry, you are not alone and, by understanding a little about how your brain works, you should be able to maximise the potential of your memory.

Most of us seem to concentrate on what we are not good at yet, if we focus on our strengths, we can attack those weaknesses.

Look at this questionnaire and grade yourself 1 to 5 (5 being excellent).

	1	2	3	4	5
How good are you at:					
Remembering facts?					
Remembering faces?					
Remembering names?					
Remembering places visited long ago?					
Remembering events?					
Remembering tunes?					
Remembering colours on posters/pictures?					
Remembering jingles?					
Remembering what is said in lessons?					
Remembering pages of text?					
Remembering what is on study related videos?					
Remembering dates?					

Now think about a test that you have had to revise for. Write a brief description of how you revised for it, for example, *'reading my notes through the night before'*.

Next look back at your strengths as identified in the chart above. Perhaps these could be incorporated into your revision? If you are good at remembering jingles for example, should you be taping notes and/or making up some 'catchy' words to go with the facts you are trying to remember? Suppose you had to remember that a useful property of beryllium is that if a nucleus does catch a fast neutron it gives off two more. As a result neutrons are multiplied in a fusion bomb. Why not try remembering it by:

Beryllium-bomb-multiplied neutron

These quick ways of remembering something are known as memory aids, or **memaids**.

MEMAIDS

Why do we remember jingles? In most cases it's because they're annoyingly 'catchy'. 'Memaids' are simple, catchy ways of aiding your memory in a similar way. For example, you can remember how to wire a plug by this memaid:

'The b**L**ue wire goes to the **L**eft and the b**R**own wire goes to the **R**ight'.

Now try making up memaids for the following two pieces of information. Use drawings instead of words if you wish.

1. Comets are collections of ice, gas and dust which orbit the Sun and reflect its light. They have highly elliptical orbits which bring them close to the Sun and then far out in the solar system.

   Memaid

2. Euxenite is a brilliant black mineral whose name comes from the Greek meaning 'friendly to strangers'.

   Memaid

Your memory works well if it can link thoughts, ideas and information. For example, give yourself three minutes to memorise this list of words in the right order: *be, and, but, so, for, it, they, maybe, if, then, the, when, because, to, not*.

Now try the same exercise with this list: *tree, green, teacher, book, van, flower, sandwich, TV, pineapple, table, butter, curtain, chocolate, bun, apple*.

Which list did you remember best? Probably the second. This is because you can visualise and link these words. You can even turn them into a story: Under the tree, the grass is green, a teacher reads a book. Her van - with a large flower painted on it, is nearby. As she eats a sandwich she wishes she had her TV there. She picks out a pineapple, sets up her table, drops the melted butter on the curtain that is her tablecloth and sets out her chocolate bun and an apple from the tree.

It's a story you could actually draw so it can be even more easily remembered.

Now select a piece of information from one of your subjects that you need to remember and devise your own *memaid*.

WHAT SORT OF STUDENT IS THIS?

Perhaps you like to listen to information rather than read it. You may prefer discussion groups to working alone or do better at exams than coursework. Identifying what you do and don't like and what you can and can't do will help identify targets for improvement.

Look at this student profile.

	Poor 1	2	3	4	Excellent 5
Listening		✓			
Analysis	✓				
Revision	✓				
Note making		✓			
Essay writing				✓	
Time management	✓				
Evaluation				✓	
Reliability		✓			
Concentration		✓			
Discussion					✓
Presentation			✓		
Research			✓		
Information technology				✓	

Using the profile above, write a list of recommendations for the student in order to strengthen some of their weaker skills. Choose two skills to start with.

Skill _____

> **I suggest you**

Skill _____

> **I suggest you**

Next, look at the student's 'best' skill or skills. How might this/these be used in order to strengthen the weaker skills?

Finally, explain how this student could build on their strengths (the areas where they scored 4 or 5).

STUDY SKILLS AUDIT

Name _____ Date _____

Rate yourself at the following study skills

	Poor 1	2	3	4	Excellent 5
Listening					
Analysis					
Revision					
Note making					
Essay writing					
Time management					
Evaluation					
Reliability					
Concentration					
Discussion					
Presentation					
Research					
Information technology					

Skill to improve _____

Target date _____

Action: what will I do to meet my target?

How will I know that I have met my target?

IMPROVING YOUR LEARNING   Section 1 – 7

LEARNING STYLES

What sort of a learner are you?
- Are you an **Action Learner** with an enthusiastic approach to new ideas, situations and learning techniques?
- Are you a **Practical Learner** who enjoys turning theory into practice and responds to challenges?
- Perhaps you are a **Thinker** and like to consider the whole situation and its possible outcomes before deciding how to approach a task.
- Or you might be a **Rationalist** who scientifically and objectively questions how ideas and situations are linked.

How might each of the above 'types' respond to the following situation? Match the four responses to the four different types of learner above.

> **You have an hour to go before your party when there is a power-cut.**
>
> 1. Make a list of all possible courses of action and list the advantages and disadvantages of each.
>   _____
>
> 2. Borrow some candles and a battery powered stereo so the party can go ahead.
>   _____
>
> 3. Immediately decide to change the theme of the party to 'murder in the dark'.
>   _____
>
> 4. Make a diagram of the electrical circuits in the house and neighbourhood to locate the source of the power cut.
>   _____

Which of those reactions would be closest to your own? What sort of learner does that suggest you might be? _____

Try to think of one *advantage* and one *disadvantage* of being that type of learner. Discuss this with a partner if you can.

Advantage _____

_____

Disadvantage _____

_____

Now think of a task set in one of your subjects.

_____

Plan to tackle it using every one of the above approaches (action, practical, thinker, rationalist) as the 'ideal' style will involve *each* of the four approaches!

BRAINSTORMING

What is it? A headache? A brainwave? It's easiest to identify what brainstorming is by learning about what it is not.

- It is *not* just a spider diagram of ideas.
- It is *not* a collection of good ideas.
- It is *not* a collection of careful thoughts, put together over an hour or so.

Even so, each of the above strategies are often claimed to be brainstorms.

So, you may ask, what is brainstorming?

It is simply a technique used for recalling old ideas, releasing a flow of new ideas and coming up with creative solutions to problems.

Brainstorming is carried out within a given short time and can be verbal or written, individual or within groups. There are no limits as to how many contributions each person can make.

It is not confined to *good* ideas. It is about generating as many spontaneous suggestions as possible, regardless of how sensible, ridiculous, stimulating or boring they are. (Any ridiculous ideas can be crossed out later, but at the time they are actually helping other ideas form.)

Research on brainstorming has shown that, as the flow of ideas declines, just one or two main ideas are usually focused on, often the most important.

Here is the start of a brainstorm on **euthanasia**. Continue this brainstorm for two minutes.

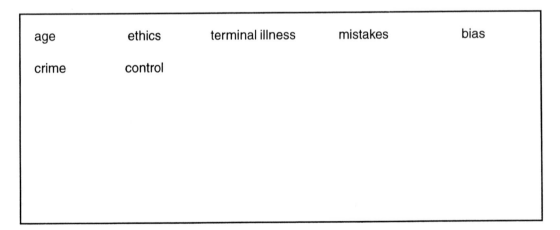

Now cross out all the words that do not seem relevant.

Identify one or two main ideas and related sub-headings from the brainstorm. Number the points to show the order in which you would use them if you were writing about euthanasia.

Try your own brainstorm.

Time allowed: two minutes. Topic: *Organising yourself for effective study*

Now reduce the brainstorm to one or two main ideas and related sub-topics.

Finally use brainstorming to help with a task set in one of your subjects.

Task _____

_____

Brainstorm

Select the most important ideas, prioritise them, decide how you will tackle the task and set yourself a time limit – now you're on the way!

THINKING ABOUT THINKING: PROBLEM SOLVING

Have you ever looked at a question or task and thought, *'Help! What does it mean? What is it asking me to do?'* Panic is a common reaction but there is a more productive response.

A problem, however complex, can be broken down into manageable proportions. Let's look at some written tasks with a view to simplifying them by using a problem solving approach.

> **Task 1**
> 'In Chartres Cathedral the Mappa Mundi labyrinth designs can be found.'
> Where did this pattern occur before the 13th century?
>
> **Task 2**
> There is an old song called 'Green Grow The Rushes-O' which refers to the 'rivals', the 'proud walkers' and 'the April rainer' as well as, amongst other things, the 'symbols' at your door, the 'bright shiner' and the 'seven stars in the sky'. Try and explain these words.

Now take *Tasks 1 and 2* and devise some questions. For example, in the first task we might raise these:

- What are labyrinth designs?
- Where is Chartres Cathedral?
- What or where is Mappa Mundi?
- What is the main point of the question?

Add some questions of your own for *Task 2*. Write down as many as you can.

Raising questions helps you tackle tasks as it helps you identify:

- What information you need to find out.
- Whether there are words you don't know the meaning of.
- The main point of the task.
- How one point relates to another.
- What steps you need to take in order to answer the question.
- What you know already.

A **flow chart** is also a useful way of solving problems. Here is an example using *Task 1*.

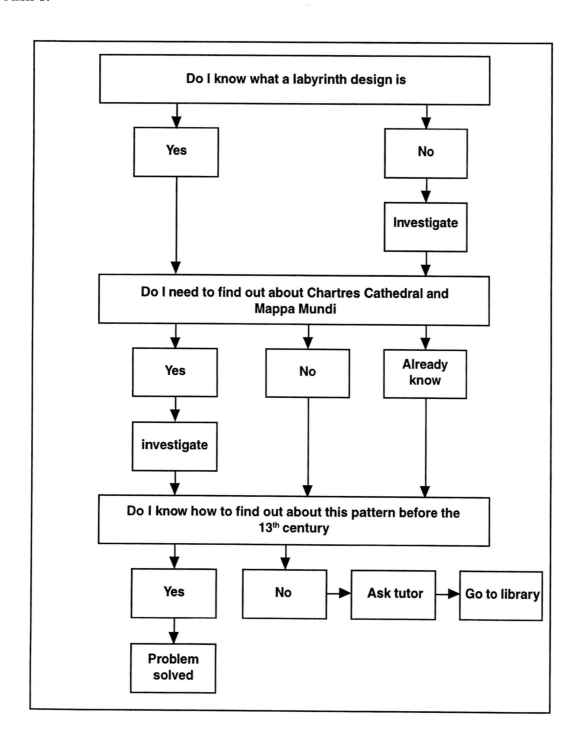

Use a question from one of your subject areas to produce a similar flow chart.

SOLVING STUDY PROBLEMS

Are you good at predicting study problems? It's a good idea to look out for and predict potential troublespots. For example, if you have ever thought, *'I never manage to do this well'* or *'Oh no, I've never understood that'*, then you are at stage one of problem solving: you have identified the problem.

Think about one area of your studies that you know causes problems. It can be in the area of **knowledge**, for example, *'I have never worked out the difference between mean, median and mode.'* Or it can be in the area of **skills**, for example, *'I just can't listen and take notes at the same time.'* Maybe it relates to your **attitudes**. You just can't seem to get sufficiently motivated to settle down to work at home.

Identify one study related problem that you know you need to sort out.

[ ]

Good. Remember that efficient problem solving starts with recognising that a problem actually exists.

Now, since we all need to be motivated in order to tackle a problem, it is important to know why you want to tackle it.

What's in it for you if you manage to tackle your problem? For example, if your problem had been listening and note taking at the same time and you overcame this, your answer to the question might be, *'I will save time copying up others' notes, I will be able to revise more efficiently, I will feel better about myself.'*

Look at your problem and fill in this box:

What's in it for me if I tackle the problem?

[ ]

OK, next you need to attack the problem. This area will need some careful thinking. Most of us, having identified a problem, set out to solve it as if we have some heavy anchor attached to us that doesn't allow us to travel back and find its root. What is needed is some serious self-analysis. This might allow us to come up with a whole variety of ideas.

IMPROVING YOUR LEARNING

Section 1 – 13

Problem: *Note taking and listening at the same time*

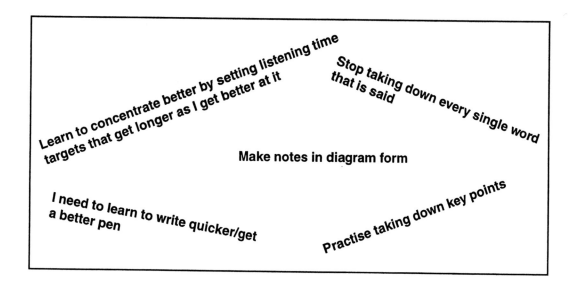

- Learn to concentrate better by setting listening time targets that get longer as I get better at it
- Stop taking down every single word that is said
- Make notes in diagram form
- I need to learn to write quicker/get a better pen
- Practise taking down key points

Remember, your solutions may involve enlisting the help of a teacher so you might also have ideas such as '*make an appointment with ...*'

Make sure the ideas you come up with are **realistic** and **achievable**.

OK. Now it's your turn. Refer back to your identified problem and come up with some ideas for dealing with it here.

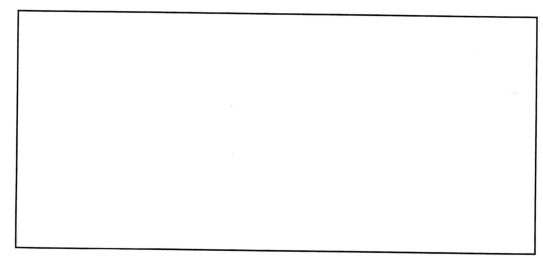

In order to be sure you really *do* something about the problem (rather than just write down your good intentions), work within a time limit by adding a date by which you intend to have attacked the problem.

Problem to be attacked by _____

© **CONNECT** Publications 1999

IMPROVING YOUR LEARNING   Section 1 – 14

SOLVING A STUDY PROBLEM

Name _____ Date _____

Problem

[ ]

What's in it for me?

[ ]

Plan of attack

[ ]

Deadline _____

© **CONNECT** Publications 1999

TIME MANAGEMENT

Do you always leave work until the last minute? And sometimes beyond? Do you experience long periods of inactivity followed by sudden panics which mean that work never reflects your best effort? If your answer is 'yes' to any of these questions then it's worth having a think about the way you organise your time.

Have you ever considered making timetables to help you organise your time? Most students need two, a *Short Term Timetable* for an immediate picture of what you need to be doing and a *Long Term Timetable* that reminds you of how many weeks or months there are to the examinations or some other major deadline.

The *Long Term Timetable* is rather like a wall planner and should be placed clearly where you will look at it regularly. Cross off each day as it passes - this is a good way to remind yourself that *'another day has gone'*.

February	March	April	May	June
1 2 3 4 5 6 7	1 2 3 4 5 6 7	1 2 3 4	1 2	1 2 3 4 5 6
8 9 10 11 12 13 14	8 9 10 11 12 13 14	5 6 7 8 9 10 11	3 4 5 6 7 8 9	7 8 9 10 11 12 13
15 16 17 18 19 20 21	15 16 17 18 19 20 21	12 13 14 15 16 17 18	10 11 12 13 14 15 16	14 15 16 17 18 19 20
22 23 24 25 26 27 28	22 23 24 25 26 27 28	19 20 21 22 23 24 25	17 18 19 20 21 22 23	21 22 23 24 25 26 27
	29 30 31	26 27 28 29 30	24 25 26 27 28 29 30	28 29 30
			31	

EXAMS

Here is an example of a *Short Term Timetable*. Fill in the dates for the next three weeks. This will involve looking at a calendar or diary, thus helping you to be a little more aware of the passage of time.

Monday	Tuesday	Wednesday	Thursday	Friday	Saturday	Sunday
Monday	Tuesday	Wednesday	Thursday	Friday	Saturday	Sunday
Monday	Tuesday	Wednesday	Thursday	Friday	Saturday	Sunday

IMPROVING YOUR LEARNING

Now, highlight the deadline dates that you have to meet during that time.

Take one of those deadline requirements and write it down here, for example: *'In five days time I need to write a 1000 word essay for History'*.

[   ]

Next, brainstorm all the tasks you have to do in order to meet the deadline, for example: *make notes, see teacher, visit library*.

Task brainstorm

Look at your brainstorm and write your plan of attack in sequence.

1. _____ 2. _____
3. _____ 4. _____
5. _____ 6. _____

This gives you some idea of the amount of time you need to allocate in order to meet your deadline. Using your sequence plan you can now allocate a time and date to each task. Be realistic, don't plan to work on days you are out or have some other engagement.

SHORT TERM TIMETABLE

Name _____

Every two weeks transfer the last week onto a new *Short Term Timetable* and fill in the rest. Pin your *Short Term Timetable* up somewhere at home where you can easily refer to it.

Monday	Monday	Monday (last week)
Tuesday	Tuesday	Tuesday
Wednesday	Wednesday	Wednesday
Thursday	Thursday	Thursday
Friday	Friday	Friday
Saturday	Saturday	Saturday
Sunday	Sunday	Sunday

USING TEACHERS' COMMENTS

What sort of work gets top marks? What exactly are teachers looking for?

Tick which of the following you think are likely to help gain high marks.

Work that has:	(✓)
Clearly identified the task	
Little clear structure or organisation	
Organised the information	
Shown thought and reflection	
A lot of detail but no analysis	
Supported main ideas with evidence/examples	
Shown no evidence of reading or research	
Developed each idea	
Met the deadline	
Mostly been copied	
Is well researched but has not completed the task set	
Considered only one point of view	

In order to get good marks it's important to use your teachers' comments in an active way. Comments are far more useful than grades alone. For example, a grade D only tells us that we are not doing well enough for an A, B or C yet are better than an E!

Take two or three pieces of recently marked work from one of your subjects.

Write the teachers' comments here.

Comments

IMPROVING YOUR LEARNING

Now look at each list and consider which are the most important to work on. Number them in order of priority.

1. _____
2. _____
3. _____
4. _____
5. _____

Write here five actions you could take in order to improve your work. Some have been suggested for you:

1. *Ask for an 'ideal' essay to look at.*
2. *Ask for the essay to be commented on at the draft stage.*
3. _____
4. _____
5. _____

Finally, read these tutor comments and write next to them if you think the work got a *low, medium* or *high* mark.

	Low	Medium	High
I can see that you have written all you know but this does not address the question.			
Your comments and research are commendable. You will need to pay attention to your punctuation in the future.			
Your work develops the argument well and I am pleased to see that you address the wider issues and implications of the question.			
You have made some attempt to support your argument which is a vast improvement.			
Your work is often of an extremely high standard yet if you do not meet set deadlines I will not accept it in the future.			
Some original ideas, well constructed and revealing a good understanding of the topic.			
You seem to have handed in a copy of my teaching notes!			

Section 2

WORKING WITH OTHERS

Teachers' notes
2.1   Similarities and differences
2.3   Listening to others
2.5   Analysing groups
2.7   Roles in groups
2.8   Body language in groups
2.10 Group dynamics
2.11 Group work evaluation

Teachers' notes
WORKING WITH OTHERS

Working with others is becoming an increasingly important aspect of study. However, co-operative working skills are often taken for granted. This section aims to promote effective group work.

Similarities and differences is designed to raise awareness that each of us brings different experiences to a situation and it is these experiences that mould our attitudes, beliefs and behaviour. Discussion and comparison of past experiences help students become aware that working with other people involves recognising and respecting their identities and presentations of self. Further discussion could be based on the reasons why we need to learn to listen to others' viewpoints, as well as contributing our own, in order for group communication to be effective.

Listening to others starts from a broad perspective, encouraging students to think about why they listen to some people more than others. (Trust, respect and a willingness to balance what otherwise might be one's own very limited viewpoint.) Students are asked to think about situations when their contribution has not been listened to and how that made them feel. Ten school or college situations in which they are required to listen may include: *the fire alarm, in a lecture, to examination starting details, in a presentation, when people are taking it in turn to read, to safety instructions.* Hopefully they will also include *'when in a group discussion'*. The next activity asks the student to list ten ways which show they have listened. The suggestions here may include *nodding, taking notes, asking for a point to be extended, offering a different viewpoint, smiling, asking for a point to be clarified or for the source of the speaker's information.* If possible, emphasise the importance of being an active listener and how it feels to the speaker when they are receiving positive feedback.

Analysing groups focuses on self analysis within the group situation. Students are encouraged to be aware of the purpose and intended outcome of any group work as well as the importance of setting time targets for discussion. If a group decides that *'by 10.30 we will have a summary of our group differences'* they are more likely to keep on task.

Roles in groups asks students to think about what makes an effective group. They extend a list of roles that one might play within a group. The extension list might include: *someone who clarifies the ideas offered, group organiser, selector of main ideas and key points, outcome manager.* Students can also make a list of roles that people might play in order to ensure an *unsuccessful* group. For example, *opter out, displacement officer, off the point person, missed the point person, why am I here? person* and so on.

Body language. Controlling non-verbal communication is a key ingredient in working effectively with others across a range of situations. Here eye contact is used as an example and students are encouraged to consider both positive and negative non verbal communication. There is a wealth of opportunity for role play follow up activities with students using body language only to communicate moods, beliefs and feelings.

Group dynamics involves thinking about the complexity of the two-way channels involved in a small group of four and then six people. Prior to handing out the sheet it is useful to ask students to try and work out for themselves how many channels of communication there are in a group of four if every person is to communicate with each of the others in the group. Students could work in pairs and feed back their answers to the whole group. They are then asked to work out how many channels of communication there are in a group of six. (The answer is 30 two-way channels.) When considering the effectiveness of different group sizes students might think about teaching and learning situations, problem solving, learning a skill, being in a sports team. Discussion could centre on how and why groups really 'work'.

Group work evaluation. Students will benefit from reflecting on their own behaviour within a group and can use this as a basis for targeting areas for improvement. Alternatively the sheet could be filled in prior to participating in a number of group activities and the *before* and *after* results compared.

WORKING WITH OTHERS

SIMILARITIES AND DIFFERENCES

Studying is not always an isolated individual activity, there are likely to be many occasions when you need to co-operate. In fact, learning is often most effective when shared. But working well with others requires skills, just like all aspects of study.

First of all you need to give everybody the respect they deserve, however different from you they appear to be.

Have you ever liked or disliked someone from the moment that you first met? It's all to do with the way a person presents themselves and your own prejudices and preconceptions.

To work well with others you need to recognise the similarities and differences that exist between you and them.

Complete these sentences:

When I meet new people I usually _____

When I don't understand something I _____

When I have a problem I usually _____

When I need someone to listen I _____

At school/college my personality is _____

At home my personality is _____

I am most happy when I am _____

I do not like it when I _____

If possible, compare your answers with a partner's. Discuss the differences.

But what about similarities?

Make a list of past experiences that are common to most students. For example, *'I went to school'*.

WORKING WITH OTHERS

Now, list some experiences that are 'unique' to you.
For example, *I am an only child*

As you can see, you're broadly similar to many other students as well as uniquely different!

LISTENING TO OTHERS

Is anybody out there listening? It's important to feel that somebody is.

Who are you most likely to go to when you need someone to listen?

Which people are you most likely to talk to in the following situations? Choose from the list below. Add some more of your own if you wish.

```
Buying new clothes _____
Having a personal problem _____
Needing a shoulder to cry on _____
Changing hairstyle _____
Feeling stressed _____
Having problems with my studies _____
Sharing a secret _____
Feeling confused _____
```

Teacher	Grandparent	Friend	Brother
Sister	Father	Mother	Neighbour
Male friend	Female friend	Boy/Girlfriend	Other (specify)

You might have found that it's not always the obvious person that you take problems to. For example, you might take a study problem to an older brother rather than a tutor. Indeed you might take all the above problems to the same person because they listen well and make you feel better.

Have you ever been telling someone something important and found they suddenly walked off to do something else or even said *'What did you say?'* as you had finished pouring your heart out?

People that take the time to *listen* show that they value you and consider you worth giving some time to – they care.

When we speak we expect people to listen rather than just hope that they do. Listening however is not a skill that we are always good at.

Write down ten college situations when you need to listen.

1. _____
2. _____
3. _____
4. _____
5. _____
6. _____
7. _____
8. _____
9. _____
10. _____

Was it difficult to think of ten situations? If so, perhaps it's because we don't often stop and think about listening – we accept that we 'just do it'.

One of the situations above could have been 'when I am working in a group during a lesson'.

This is an important listening situation.

Think about a situation at college when you might need to communicate in a group. How could you show others in the group that you were listening to them? List as many ways as you can think.

If you can, compare your list with another student's.

Do you use all these methods? How can you improve your listening skills?

WORKING WITH OTHERS   Section 2 – 5

ANALYSING GROUPS

Working in groups is not easy so it's worth spending some time thinking about what creates effective group working and about how we behave in groups.

Successful groups

Think of situations in the present or past when you have found group or team work useful and rewarding. It could be with a group of friends or in a club, organisation or team.

[   ]

These successful group situations are likely to have had a *sense of purpose*. You need to know *why* you are in the group, *want* to be a part of it and have identified what group *outcome* is intended.

Groups put together for study purposes need to define these things at the start of their discussion.

Think of the last study group situation you took part in.

What was the purpose of the group and what was the intended outcome?

[   ]

(If you can't remember easily, is it because you were, to put it politely, not an active member of the group?)

Responsibilities of group members

Tick which of these you've ever done when put into a group situation to work - go on - be honest.

I have talked about things other than the topic	
I have not offered any ideas	
I have found it a good opportunity to catch up on homework	
I let the others get on with it	
Anything else?	

© **CONNECT** Publications 1999

WORKING WITH OTHERS

Just think what would happen if each group member let the others get on with it .....
yes, it would be a quiet group if nothing else.

Everyone in a group needs to be actively involved for the group to be successful and for everyone to get the most out of it. Below is a list of some of the ways group members need to be actively involved.

Think of a recent occasion when you were asked to be work as part of a group and 'grade' yourself on each aspect, five being excellent and one being very poor.

	Poor				Excellent
Turn taking	1	2	3	4	5
Offering ideas	1	2	3	4	5
Listening	1	2	3	4	5
Extending others' ideas	1	2	3	4	5
Offering alternative ideas	1	2	3	4	5
Justifying comments	1	2	3	4	5
Respecting others' comments	1	2	3	4	5

Finally think of any group situation that you know of, or have been part of, that could be considered successful.

Write down five reasons for the success of the group. If possible, compare your observations with a fellow student.

1. _____

2. _____

3. _____

4. _____

5. _____

ROLES IN GROUPS

Have you ever been in a group situation where no one knew what to say?
Have you ever been in a group situation where everyone had too much to say?
What about when one person does all the talking and doesn't give you a chance to say a word?

Other problems can arise if group members don't focus on their task. Unless each member of the group is 'on task' a discussion becomes a diversion!

Here is a task that a group was trying to focus on. Grade the comments below according to their relevance.

Task: *Should there be a pool table in the student common room?*

	not at all relevant				very relevant
1. 'Many students would really enjoy that'	1	2	3	4	5
2. 'I think with so many students here we need two'	1	2	3	4	5
3. 'I don't play pool'	1	2	3	4	5
4. 'Whoever goes to the student common room?'	1	2	3	4	5
5. 'Yes, and a television and video'	1	2	3	4	5
6. 'Has anyone done the last essay?'	1	2	3	4	5

Do you recognise that sort of discussion? How could you possibly decide what the outcome of the discussion was? What went wrong?

One way of avoiding these situations is to make sure each group member is aware of the many roles they have to play in order to be part of an effective group.

Here are some group roles – add some more if you can and circle those you know you 'play' when involved in group discussion:

chairperson	note taker	initiator of ideas	developer of ideas
listener	summariser	evaluator	time manager
'keeping on task' manager	adviser	questioner	builder of ideas

Another way of avoiding group chaos is to get off to a good start by making clear how the group is going to work – setting out some basic rules.

Make a list of four basic rules that will help a group complete its task effectively.

1. _____
2. _____
3. _____
4. _____

BODY LANGUAGE IN GROUPS

It's estimated that we communicate a lot more through our bodies than our words. What silent messages do you give and receive?

Have you felt uncomfortable because someone is staring at you for example?

Staring is OK for museums and aquaria, but staring at a person reduces them to an object!

So what's the difference between staring and simply gaining eye contact?

Let's see what you think. Fill in the right hand column.

Action	This means:
You gain eye contact with someone speaking and nod	_____
You look right away from a speaker	_____
A speaker gains eye contact with you	_____
A speaker fixes her/his look at you	_____

Our eyes, together with the position of our body and the angle of our head, give feedback that indicates how we feel about ourselves, others and the situations we're in.

Think of the body language you might see in a classroom. List four examples which would give the impression of lack of interest, boredom and not caring about the work.

1. _____
2. _____
3. _____
4. _____

Now give four examples which give the impression of interest and enthusiasm

1. _____
2. _____
3. _____
4. _____

WORKING WITH OTHERS   Section 2 – 9

The way a room is laid out and your position in it can also communicate quite a lot.

A small group tutorial is taking place. The first two students arrive and choose where to sit. What impression is the tutor likely to get in each case and what might the two students be thinking?

	Tutor			Tutor			Tutor	
			Student	Student		Student		
Student	Student						Student	

Tutor thinks	Tutor thinks	Tutor thinks

Students think	Students think	Students think

Draw how the furniture could have been arranged in order to ensure that everyone felt 'equal' in the situation and was not faced with awkward decisions about where to sit.

© **CONNECT** Publications 1999

WORKING WITH OTHERS   Section 2 – 10

GROUP DYNAMICS

Have you ever been in a group where you waited for your opportunity to contribute but it just never came?

It's really frustrating, especially when you know you had a really good idea to share.

If you understand the complexity of group sizes it explains quite a lot.

Within a successful group each member might reasonably be expected to listen and reply to each of the others, this is what happens in a group with four members:

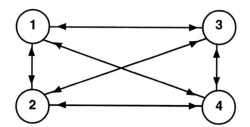

How many two-way channels of communication can you count in this group of four? _ _ _ _ _

Now, here is a group of six people.
Work out how many two-way channels of communication there are here.

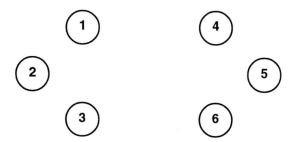

In a group of six there are _ _ _ _ _ channels of two-way communication.

Now you can see why the larger a group is the harder it is for everyone to speak to each other.

Using your knowledge of group dynamics, think of some school or college situations where smaller or larger groups are most effective.

small groups (2-9) most effective   *large groups (10 and over) most effective*

© CONNECT Publications 1999

GROUP WORK EVALUATION

Think of the last time you were required to work in a group.

What was the group task? _ _ _ _ _ _ _ _ _ _ _ _ _ _ _ _ _ _

Mark how effective you feel you were at these group skills.

	Totally unsuccessful				Totally successful
Keeping awake	1	2	3	4	5
Supporting other's views	1	2	3	4	5
Turn taking	1	2	3	4	5
Offering a different view	1	2	3	4	5
Extending ideas	1	2	3	4	5
Keeping on task	1	2	3	4	5
Listening to others	1	2	3	4	5
Respecting other's views	1	2	3	4	5
What other skills did you use?					
_ _ _ _ _ _ _ _ _ _ _ _ _ _ _ _ _ _	1	2	3	4	5
_ _ _ _ _ _ _ _ _ _ _ _ _ _ _ _ _ _	1	2	3	4	5
Now evaluate the success of the group itself					
Time management	1	2	3	4	5
Allocation of roles	1	2	3	4	5
Organisation	1	2	3	4	5
Keeping on task	1	2	3	4	5
Quality of outcome	1	2	3	4	5

Explain how you think the quality of the group work could have been improved.

Section 3

READING

Teachers' notes
3.1 Preparing to read
3.3 Reading with a sense of purpose (1)
3.4 Reading with a sense of purpose (2)
3.5 Changing words to pictures
3.7 SQ3R
3.9 Skimming, rapid reading and scanning

Teachers' notes
READING

Many students experience problems in reading for study purposes. This section emphasises the importance of taking a practical approach to the development of reading skills.

Preparing to read asks the student to take time to familiarise him or herself with a text rather than find out about its content as they go along. A useful extension activity is to ask students to refer to any of their current textbooks and spend five minutes reading only the introductory sentence of each paragraph of a chapter they have not yet studied. Students studying from more visual texts (for example, from the sciences) should look at the illustrations only. They should then write a paragraph explaining what they think the chapter is about.

Reading with a sense of purpose: reading through headings engages students in an active approach to reading that will help them retain meaning as it engages the long term memory. Students may extend this activity by reversing the process. They can select text or a page of a newspaper and read only the headings or sub-headings before writing a short paragraph explaining what they think the text is about. They can then read the text fully and judge how effective the headings were in predicting the text content.

Reading with a sense of purpose: reading by asking questions encourages students to develop an enquiring mind when faced with a new text. The activity could be concluded by asking students to formulate ten questions they could mentally ask of a new text. For example, who wrote it? What is it about? What is the author's intention? What does it aim to tell me? When was it written? Is it fiction or non-fiction? Why am I reading it? Do I need to remember it?

Changing words to pictures is an excellent technique for note making (see section on *Note making and note taking*) but is not used in that context here. The technique can also be a very important part of active reading. By involving as many senses as possible the reader interacts with the text as a whole rather than merely with the act of decoding. Students maintain that *reading and doing* really helps them remember text details. As an extension activity, ask students to imagine any actual person included in their studies. Ask them to draw that person in a fairly detailed way - cartoon type drawings work very well. Now ask them to colour the drawing. The character drawn should, from now on, always represent that person when they read about him/her. Students can then draw a speech balloon and write a comment or idea attributed to that person. Discuss how, by bringing a name to life and making it a real person, silent reading can become visual.

The **SQ3R** method of reflective reading (taken from the SRA reading laboratory) is a higher order reading skill that can assist efficient reading. It uses three aspects of memory: registration, retention and retrieval, and gives a structure to reading a text that enables recall. It is important to remind students that they should formulate a bank of questions before reading to answer them and not simply make up a question and then immediately read to answer it. Discuss when students think this approach to reading would be most useful (for example, when revising or when faced with a new text).

Skimming, rapid reading and scanning. This activity asks students to consider the importance of a 'rapid read' of text in order to 'warm up' to its content. Scanning involves the eyes scanning backwards and forwards as they read sentences out of sequence in their search for meaning. An activity approach to scanning is to ask the students to mark out their eye movements of the areas of text they scan with a coloured pen. For example, they might mark the tenth sentence, then move to the third, then the first, then the sub-heading. This visual scan approach emphasises the importance of the backward and forward reading approach in building up a mental picture of content.

PREPARING TO READ

Athletes *warm up* their bodies before physical activity. Reading also benefits from *warming up*. By preparing the brain for the study of a book in a similar way to preparing the body prior to physical activity, you can evaluate the text in terms of print, language and use of illustrations. This process is known as ***pre-reading***.

Pre-reading has a number of uses. It can:
- help you find your way around a text prior to using it
- enable you to see what areas you are already familiar with and which are completely new
- help you get used to the layout of a book - for example, some texts contain summary boxes and example pages
- familiarise you with the language in a book, allowing you to judge how simple or difficult it is.

In this example you have been given only:
a. The chapter heading
b. The opening sentence
c. The final paragraph

> a. A Harm Reduction Approach: Limiting Damage to the Community
>
> b. There is a growing recognition that containment rather than elimination of drug misuse is the more realistic objective.
>
> c. In practice this approach has resulted in the development of a variety of interventions which seek to influence different levels of drug misuse. These include outreach work, needle and syringe exchange, prescribing services, local prevention campaigns etc. We believe that a similar hierarchy of goals could be applied to the policing context.

Now write two sentences explaining what the text extract is about.

Next, take a text book from any subject you study. Select three chapters from the book that you have not yet read.

Note down any sub-headings and titles. Look at any diagrams or illustrations. Read the introductory paragraph and summary.

Allow yourself only six minutes per chapter.

Now write a summary of all you have worked out about the content of these chapters.

Book title

Chapter numbers or titles

First chapter

Second chapter

Third chapter

READING WITH A SENSE OF PURPOSE (1)

Reading through headings

Do you ever read a section of writing again and again but still fail to remember what it's all about? If so, it may be because your reading doesn't really have enough of a sense of purpose for it to be retained in your long term memory. But how can you develop a greater sense of purpose? Try this exercise.

Here is an extract about guitar making. Write a sub-heading or *label* for each paragraph. The first has been done for you.

Craftsmanship
The best guitars are made by individual craftsmen using the finest woods available. Little machinery is employed and usually each craftsman involved makes one or two parts with the final assembly being completed by someone with that individual expertise.

_ _ _ _ _ _ _ _ _ _ _ _ _ _ _ _ _ _ _
Each part of the guitar is usually made from a different wood. The side and back is made of rosewood, the finger board of ebony, the neck of cedar or mahogany and the top of Alpine spruce. If possible it is advisable to buy a spruce topped guitar where the lines of the grain are evenly spaced.

_ _ _ _ _ _ _ _ _ _ _ _ _ _ _ _ _ _ _
The guitar has fan-strutting under the brace which is a form of bracing. Whilst the struts were initially added for strength they do in fact produce a marked improvement in the quality of tone and are part of the standard construction technique. By reaching inside the soundhole it is possible to check the struts.

_ _ _ _ _ _ _ _ _ _ _ _ _ _ _ _ _ _ _
The standard width for the finger board is two to three inches at the nut widening to four inches at the soundhole. The fingers can be trained to these distances. It is important to ensure that the fingerboard is of sufficient width and that it is not curved.

_ _ _ _ _ _ _ _ _ _ _ _ _ _ _ _ _ _ _
The strings should not be set too high as the height determines the playing action of the guitar. If they are set too low, however, the strings will vibrate against the frets. Adjustments can be made by lowering or raising the bone pieces at the bridge and the nut.

_ _ _ _ _ _ _ _ _ _ _ _ _ _ _ _ _ _ _
Before learning how to play the guitar it is necessary to know how the fingers of each hand are referred to. The letters used for the right hand are derived from the Spanish words, *indicio* for index, *medio* for middle finger, *anular* for ring finger and *pulgar* for thumb.

In this exercise your reading was given a purpose: to identify sub-headings. Hopefully having a purpose helped you pay attention to the text, making it easier to understand and remember.

Now try the same exercise with any of the text or reference books you use.

READING WITH A SENSE OF PURPOSE (2)

Reading by asking questions

Asking questions is one of the oldest methods of teaching. It can also be a very effective method of focusing your reading. By writing your own questions on a chapter or extract you are forced to identify the main points and decide what is important to know about them.

- Read the extract below at least twice.
- Highlight the main points or arguments.
- Make up two questions about the extract for a fellow student to answer.
- Check that your questions could be successfully answered by answering them yourself.
- Change the original questions if necessary.

> Balti blues have hit the great British curry house. After 20 years of spectacular growth, a cold wind is blowing through the world of hot food and forcing restaurants out of business at the rate of three a week.
> Those in the curry trade blame increasingly sophisticated competition from supermarkets, poor service and a reluctance among second generation Anglo-Asians to run family businesses.
> The popularity of travel to the Indian sub-continent is also thought to be reponsible. People are no longer satisfied with anglicised ultra-hot curries and want to enjoy the more subtle and authentic flavours from coastal regions such as Kerala and Goa, or southern Indian vegetarian fare.
>
> *Adapted from the 'Independent on Sunday', 14th February 1999*

Your questions

Now select some passages from your textbooks. Read them in order to make up a suitable question or questions.

CHANGING WORDS TO PICTURES

You probably find it easier to understand and recall information if it is presented in a visual form of some sort – in pictures or diagrams for example. Transferring sections of text into a visual form is an excellent way of identifying key points and thinking about links between the ideas described. It will also provide you with a really useful resource for revision.

Here is an example of text that has been transformed to a more visual form.

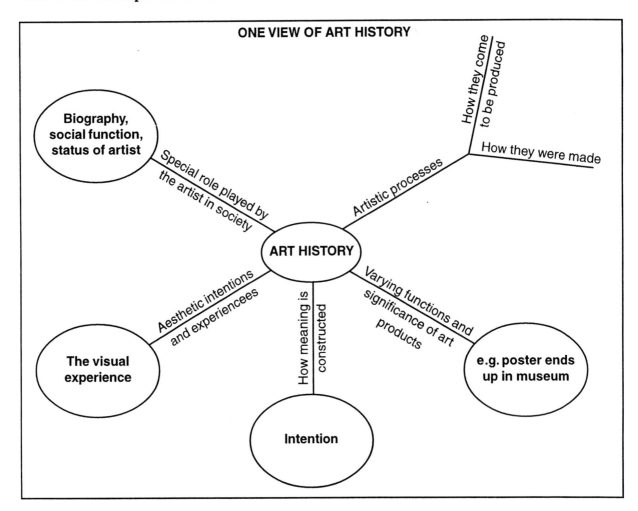

Original text

One view of art history is that it is a history of processes – artistic processes that result in the final production and other processes involved in the mechanics of how the art is produced. It is also interested in the varying functions and significance of art products, at the time they were made and also at later stages. A good example of this is the old posters that later became museum pieces, for example those promoting the London Underground.

Art history is also the history of aesthetic experience and intentions and discusses the changing appreciation of visual experience. It also looks at the function and status of the artist, asking about their background, their place in society, the reasons for their commissions and what they were trying to achieve. Art history is thus a history of how meaning is created in the visual arts.

READING
Section 3 – 6

Now, try to transform this text into your own visual form, different from the one above. Use colour and drawing as much as possible.

Creating diagrams and pictures takes less time than reading text again and again in order to remember it. It also helps the details go into your long-term memory.

Now select an extract from one of your own text books and transform it!

SQ3R

This seemingly meaningless collection of symbols is, in fact, a code which should help you to read more efficiently and more effectively. It should also be a great help during revision.

SQ3R means:
Survey the text, then formulate a
Question.
Read to answer it, then
Record your answer before finally
Reviewing what you've learned.

SQ3R is an approach to reading that – when perfected – is a very efficient method of achieving:
- faster reading
- the identification of important points
- long term retention of facts.

Put SQ3R into action. Take any one of your text books and select one chapter.

Survey
You are now going to complete a two minute survey on the chapter by glancing over any headings and sub-headings and then reading the first and last paragraphs.

Chapter summary (brief description of content of chapter)

Formulate questions
This involves taking one heading, sub-heading or main point at a time and turning each into a written question.
This is by no means straightforward so it's useful to have some practice.

Look at some examples:

The heading, 'The Necessity of Law', for example, might encourage the question, 'Give reasons why law is necessary in order for society to function'.

'Gladstone's Home Rule Bill 1886' might initiate the question, 'What were the proposals of the Bill?'

(Beware simply adding a question mark to the heading - think carefully about the value of the question.)

Now formulate some questions for these headings:

a. *Unemployment in Britain 1929-1931*
b. *The Government of Britain 1760*
c. *Magnetic Fields and Magnetic Dipoles*
d. *Tests for Identifying the Gifted Child*
e. *Steps in Using The SQ3R Method for Study*

Questions:

a. _____

b. _____

c. _____

d. _____

e. _____

OK, now back to your selected text. Formulate questions for your own text headings.

Having completed the question part of the activity, **Read** to answer each question briefly yet concisely. **Record** (write down) your answers.

Questions	Answers

Finally, **Review** the situation by looking briefly at each heading once more and reciting from memory all you now know.

SKIMMING, RAPID READING AND SCANNING

Being asked to read an article or chapter from a book does not have to be a painful struggle. Simple techniques can make it much easier. Think about newspapers. They help us take in the essentials of each article by having clear headlines and sub-headings which 'prepare' our brain for the content of the passage as we skim over them.

Skimming

Skimming involves reading headings, sub-headings and the first and last sentences, as well as looking at any illustrations and diagrams.

Take just a couple of seconds to skim the following advertisement.

> Research has validated the claim that the number of burglaries can be cut dramatically in households and establishments where property is code marked and an 'Ownership Marked' sticker is prominently displayed.
>
> Using the 'Safemate' kit you too can code mark all of your property. The Safemate pens - both fine tip and broad tip enable you to write your postcode and house number so that you and only you can check the markings with your ultra-violet Safemate Light - operated by the four Long Last batteries included in the kit. Also included are three window stickers and 12 individual warning stickers. All this is a quality hard backed wallet.

Now complete the following sentence.

The article is about

Having skimmed through the article you should have an idea if the information was any use. If not, you have not wasted any time by struggling through the whole thing.

Rapid reading

Assuming we needed to know more, the next stage would be a rapid read through.

What exactly is *rapid*? Well, the average 'normal' reading speed is likely to be between 220 and 275 words per minute and this extract contains only 108 words so – how long should you give yourself?

Rapid read the extract and answer the following questions.

What could be the title of this text?

What is it about?

_____

_____

What are its main points?

_____

_____

_____

Think about the time it took to read the text using these strategies. Do you think it would have been quicker to have read each word, as printed, in 'mechanical' order, giving each word equal weighting?

Explain what you think.

_____

_____

_____

_____

Scanning

Scanning involves reading words or sentences out of order as your eyes scan backwards and forwards through the text searching for detail.

Try this by scanning the original text looking for specific details.

Write three details below.

1. _____
2. _____
3. _____

Hopefully the *Skimming, Rapid Reading and Scanning* (SRS) approach has helped you come to terms with the extract much more quickly than just reading it over. Now you should be able to use this approach to an article or extract from your own studies.

Section 4

NOTE MAKING AND NOTE TAKING

Teachers' notes
4.1   Linear notes
4.2   Visual notes
4.4   Using key words
4.5   Taking notes from a lecture
4.7   Mind-mapping
4.8   Storyboarding
4.10 Summarising

Teachers' notes
NOTE MAKING AND NOTE TAKING

The purpose of these activities is to improve students' note making skills by introducing them to a range of techniques and encouraging them to think about the reasons for taking notes. What are they intended for? Do they succeed in those intentions?

Linear notes are the most common form of notes and are often students' preferred note taking and note making style. If this is the case, it is vital that their linear note making is effective. Students should therefore use this activity to evaluate their linear notes. They should also be encouraged to number the pages of their linear notes and keep a contents page. The reasons for this could form the basis of a class discussion. Using abbreviations and shortened word forms is an important part of producing effective linear notes. As an extension activity, ask students to shorten these words for note taking purposes: *education, classification, ministry, monopoly, objectives, behavioural, documentation, reference, technology, procedures*. They could also try abbreviating these: *therefore, in addition, note this point, greater than, less than*. Afterwards, students might think up or look up some more abbreviations that they could use in their notes.

Students who feel more at ease with linear notes should discuss in what situations alternative strategies for note taking might also be effective. They may wish to transform their linear notes to a more visual form at some later date or simply go straight into using another strategy once they have gained confidence. They will certainly manage their learning more effectively if they are aware of the full range of options available and of the contexts in which different strategies are likely to be successful.

Many students find **Visual notes** most memorable. As an extension students could select a 100 word text extract from any book they are currently using and transform it to a more visual form. Setting a time on task (try ten minutes) should encourage focused thinking. After this time students could compare their notes and discuss their effectiveness.

A possible extension for the **Key words** activity is to ask students to take one page of notes from their file and highlight each key word. Discussion might then revolve around the usefulness of the non-key words that are left.

Taking notes from a lecture should provoke discussion about when and in what form notes should be taken during a lecture or presentation. It should also provide guidance on how effective notes can be taken in these contexts. At the end of the activity the tips and helpful comments could be collected and made available to all students.

The purpose of **Mind-mapping** is to identify what is already known. Students can conclude this activity, however, by discussing how mind maps can also help them to see where there are gaps in their knowledge.

Whilst **Storyboarding** might not be a relevant form of note making for all subjects, it is important that students are aware of this strategy because many find the act of sequencing notes and information difficult. Discuss how *storyboarding* could help in writing up scientific experiments, testing hypotheses, writing a log, etc.

The **Summarising** activity provides a useful opportunity to discuss the meaning of the word *summarising* (the succinct presentation of ideas, information or opinion) and also the occasions on which summarising may be required. Since successful summarising requires the skills of comprehension, classification, definition, evaluation and selection it pervades the whole range of communication competencies and its demands should not be underestimated. As a useful extension activity ask students to consider the situations where summarising techniques are vital. Some examples could be: *summing up the news on television, passing on a telephone message in a written form, giving a verbal account of your curriculum vitae, sending a fax, drafting a circular, writing a press release*.

LINEAR NOTES

Linear notes are summaries of information presented in conventional written lines. This type of note making is very popular, especially in a classroom situation. Many students transfer their linear notes to a more visual form later, often as part of the revision process.

It's likely that there are lots of linear notes in your files. Select one page of linear notes, look at them closely and evaluate them by putting a tick or cross as appropriate by each statement.

My selected page of linear notes:

	(✓ or x)
Is clearly dated	
Is easy to read	
Is easy to select key points from	
Has clear headings	
Has clear sub-headings	
Uses abbreviations where possible	
Has numbered main points	
Has underlined main points	
Has highlighted main points	
Uses phrases rather than whole sentences	
Uses arrows to indicate the next point	
Has boxes drawn round vital points	
Uses a different colour pen for quotations	
Has a wide margin in order to note key points later	
Leaves space before a new idea	

Now take your selected page of notes and give them a 'makeover' by transforming them into 'ideal' linear notes.

Compare the 'before and after' notes. Which do you think are the most useful? Why?

VISUAL NOTES

Making successful notes involves summarising material and presenting it in a form that provides the essential points in a clear and memorable way. Information presented visually is often the easiest to remember.

Look at these visual notes and then highlight the corresponding key points in the original text, which follows.

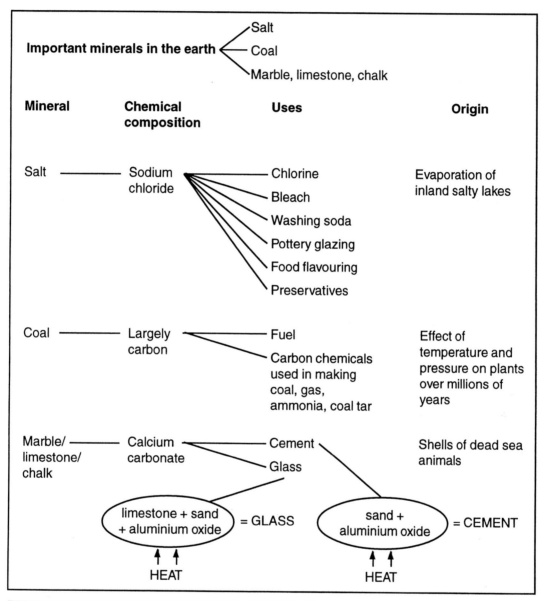

Important minerals in the earth

There are many important minerals in the earth, for example salt, whose chemical composition is sodium chloride and which originates from the evaporation of salty inland lakes. Salt is used in making chlorine, bleaches, washing soda and the glazing for pottery as well as food flavourings and preservatives.

Coal is an important mineral, both as a fuel and as a source of carbon chemicals. The composition of coal is largely carbon. Coal is used to make coke and coal gas, ammonia and coal tar. Coal originates from the effect of pressure and temperature on plants and trees over millions of years. This is why it is known as a fossil fuel.

Marble, limestone and chalk originate from the shells of dead sea animals and are made of calcium carbonate. This is used to make cement by roasting sand and aluminium oxide and glass by heating limestone with sand and aluminium oxide.

Tick which of these strategies the visual notes used.

	(✓)
Use of headings	
Use of sub-headings	
Emphasising words by underlining, capitals, and highlighting or bold print	
Linking a series of points by numbering	
Connecting related points by arrows or lines	
Using diagrams or pictures	
Leaving gaps between different points	

Add any of those summarising techniques that were not used to make the visual notes on the previous page even more effective. For example, you could number the main points.

Next, try to make your own visual notes on the following passage using as many of the techniques above as you can.

> Sea water is a source of the chemical family called halogens. Fluorine, chlorine, bromine and iodine are examples of halogens. The amount of fluorine dissolved in one cubic mile of sea water is 7,000 tonnes. Fluorine is often added to tap water to help stop tooth decay. Chlorine is commonly used to kill germs, as a bleaching agent and in the manufacture of types of plastics and insecticides. In one cubic mile of sea water the amount of chlorine dissolved is 1,000,000,000 tonnes in contrast to only 3,000,000 tonnes of bromine. Like chlorine, bromine is used in bleaching and in the eradication of germs. It is also used in the manufacture of fire extinguishers.

USING KEY WORDS

A vital part of note making is the identification of key words. These act as 'triggers' that remind you of more detail and explanation. Using a wide margin on the left hand side of your paper can really help emphasise key words and phrases.

Read this extract then note the *key words only* in the wide margin provided below.

> Most of the rocks of the earth's crust are no longer found in the position in which they were first formed or deposited as they have been subjected to tectonic forces which have deformed the original rock structures.
>
> Tectonic movements usually occur slowly over long periods of time but some, like the earthquake, take place suddenly and violently.
>
> Epeirogenic movements are relatively slow movements involving the broad uplift or submergence of extensive areas. The rock strata affected are not normally intensively folded or fractured, however they may be tilted gently or warped.

Key Words e.g. tectonic forces	

Now, in the rest of the space, briefly note the main points associated with each key word.

Try this when you are next required to take notes. Make the *Key Word* side of the sheet one third of the width of the page.

Finally, look back at the notes you have made above. Cover the key points and text and using the *Key Words* margin as your only clue, recall as much information as you can.

Hopefully you've managed to remember quite a lot. You see - good note making skills can become a useful revision aid!

NOTE MAKING AND NOTE TAKING   Section 4 – 5

TAKING NOTES FROM A LECTURE

Sometimes teachers and lecturers will expect you to take notes while they are talking. On other occasions you may be expected to take notes from a video. Although you might not always directly be told to take notes it is really common sense to keep a record of what has gone on.

Here are some reasons for taking notes. Try to add two more.

1. *To jog my memory later.*

2. *To help my understanding.*

3. *To keep me awake.*

4. _____

5. _____

Here are some comments students have made about note taking. Tick any that apply to you.

> 'If I make notes and listen at the same time I miss some of what is being said.'
>
> _____
>
> 'I can't watch a video and write things down at the same time.'
>
> _____
>
> 'I don't know what I'm supposed to note down so I try and write down all that is said.'
>
> _____
>
> 'Some words are so long I spend more time worrying about how they are spelt than about what they mean.'
>
> _____

Here is some advice about taking notes. Copy the best advice for each student under their comment above. You may repeat the same advice for more than one student if you wish. Add your own advice as well if you can.

- Summarise the key points directly at the end of the lesson or video.
- Use abbreviations for some words.
- Ask the teacher to summarise the key points at the end of each lesson.
- Number all the main points and make them the only things you write down.
- Put all the key points down in the margin and test your memory by filling in the detail at home that evening.
- Use sketches and illustrations where possible.

NOTE MAKING AND NOTE TAKING

Section 4 – 6

Read the following teachers' comments on note taking. Grade them from 1 to 5 to find out which teacher is the worst! (5 being really helpful, 1 being really lousy.)

		Grade
Mr. A	I expect my pupils to know what notes to take.	
Ms. B	I repeat certain points to give a clue as to what is important.	
Miss C	I stop every so often and hope someone writes something down.	
Mr. D.	I start the lesson by saying 'Have your note books out.'	
Mr A.	I frown at those not making notes.	
Ms. B	I talk slowly and clearly and emphasise important points.	
Miss C	I tell them to use their notes for homework at the end of the lesson.	
Mr. D	I don't think they need any notes, they should train their memory.	
Mr A	I don't, um ah, say er anything that is, actually, not um important so they should er take down my every word.	
Ms B	I summarise the key points at the end and give time for note taking at that time. I often take in notes made to see if we need some note taking lessons.	
Miss C	Every time I mark homework I can tell that most of them are no good at taking notes.	
Mr D	If they spent less time saying they don't understand and listened they wouldn't need notes.	
Mr A	I encourage those taking notes by smiling at them.	
Ms B	I give summary notes as handouts in case some points have been left out, then we go over them together so questions can be asked.	
Miss C	Pupils today just don't try.	
Mr D	I actually saw one young man drawing illustrations and charts for notes, I said 'This is not an art lesson' - he was colouring things in would you believe!	
Final scores:	Mr A _ _ _ _ Ms B _ _ _ _ Miss C _ _ _ _ Mr D _ _ _ _	

Summarise the comments of the teacher who scored the most points.

Add any other helpful comments or tips for note taking that you would pass on to a fellow student.

MIND-MAPPING

Mind-maps make very useful notes. In fact you learn a great deal just by creating them. Mind-maps work by identifying key words and then using arrows, colours, codes and pictures to illustrate connections. The main idea is centralised and other related ideas branch out from this.

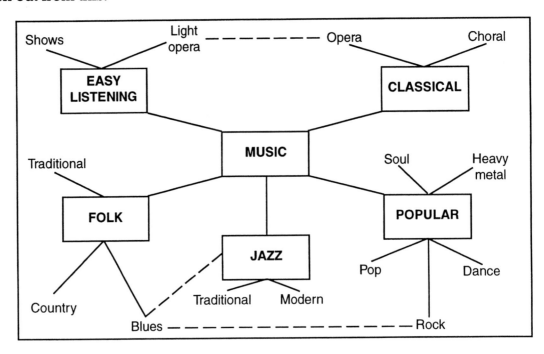

Now try filling in the gaps and making some more connections in this one.

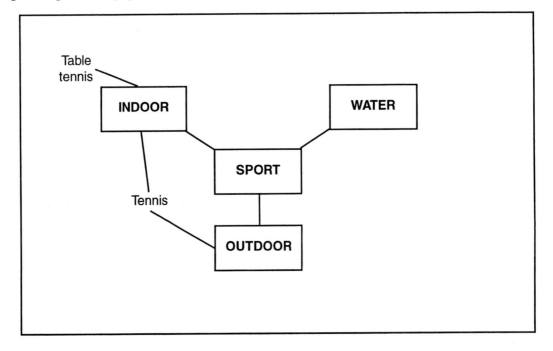

OK. Now try to make your own mind-map.
Choose any topic or question related to one of your subjects. Write it in the centre of a sheet of paper. Use colour if possible and write clearly.

Mind-mapping is not just a good way to take notes - it can also be a very useful way to revise.

STORYBOARDING

Have you ever been frustrated trying to make notes from a video or getting to grips with the organisation of a complicated book? Maybe you've forgotten what happened, when it happened and to whom it happened. Even if you've never experienced those problems, we all need to find ways of recalling and making a record of events and developments accurately and in the right sequence.

The makers of moving images use **storyboards** to give an indication of the sequence of their film or video and a quick idea of what each scene will look like. In order to create a storyboard a piece of paper is divided into a number of squares, each containing a rough picture of each scene, in sequence.

The storyboarding technique can be easily adapted to provide a simple method of recording the organisation, sequence and development of a book, film or video.

Here is an example of a storyboard for 'Gulliver's Travels' by Jonathan Swift.

Chapter 1 Gulliver restless as a doctor. Takes post as a surgeon on the Antelope.	**Chapter 2** Shipwrecked. Finds himself on Lilliput.	**Chapter 3** Pact between Gulliver and the emperor. There are seven conditions.
Chapter 4 Visits Milkendo, the capital. High heel, low heel party.	**Chapter 5** Saves them from Blefuscudian invasion. Reward: title.	**Chapter 6** Flimnap, royal treasurer, says Gulliver too expensive.

Now try and create your own storyboard for Dickens' 'The Pickwick Papers'. Here are some chapter summaries.

Chapter 1   Pickwick (as editor) introduces the meeting of the Pickwick Club, May 1827. Pickwick, Tracy Tupman, Augustus Snodgrass and Nathaniel Winkle are to travel through England and submit papers.

Chapter 2   Pickwick mistaken as an informer, rescued by Mr. Jingle. Mr. Jingle borrows Winkle's suit and angers Dr. Slammer who challenges the owner of the suit but sees that Winkle is not the man who offended him. Pickwick mistaken as an informer, rescued by Mr. Jingle. Mr. Jingle borrows Winkle's suit and angers Dr. Slammer who challenges the owner of the suit but sees that Winkle is not the man who offended him.

Chapter 3   Dismal Jemmy - Jem Huntley - is introduced to the Pickwickians. Dr. Slammer arrives and recognises Jingle and Tupman, who had been with him.

Chapter 4 Pickwick, Winkle and Snodgrass saved by Mr. Tupman's friend Mr. Wardle when caught in mock battle. Tupman flirts with Wardle's sister Rachael. Wardle invites them all to his home, 'Dingly Dell'.

Chapter 5 Dismal Jemmy promises to lend Pickwick a 'curious manuscript'. A series of accidents on the road to Dingly Dell leave Pickwick and Winkle's pride hurt.

Chapter 6 After supper the Pickwickians listen to the clergyman's tale of 'The Convict's Return'.

Chapter 1	Chapter 2	Chapter 3
Chapter 4	Chapter 5	Chapter 6

Without referring to the storyboard, try to answer the following questions.

- Who borrows Winkle's suit?
- What tale does the clergyman tell?
- In which chapter does a series of accidents occur?
- What is Jem Huckley's nickname?
- Who are to submit papers?
- How many characters have we been introduced to in these first six chapters?

Hopefully you will have been able to answer most of these questions simply through creating a storyboard.

SUMMARISING

How useful are your notes when it comes to revision? The most useful notes are likely to be:
- concise
- comprehensive
- clear.

A key factor in successful note making is to realise that you don't have to write down every word, only the most important.

Read the following set of student notes. Then cross out as many words as you can while still leaving notes that cover all the key points.

REPORTS

All organisations use reports. Every day they have to give reports in the form of written or verbal accounts of something. Reports fall into two broad categories which are routine reports and special reports.

Routine reports are reports that supply information about normal business matters or professional matters. The purpose of these reports is so well known and they are used so often that a form for routine reports may have been designed. If so this routine report form just has to be filled in. Sometimes routine reports are part of the employees regular routine and they are told in advance when these routine reports should be submitted.

Special reports are used when some special problem or interest arises. That is why they are called *special:* their purpose is unique to the problem or the situation.

Routine reports usually have their purpose clearly defined in advance.

How many words could you cross out and still understand the content?
There are 155 words in the original notes. You could actually have crossed out at least half.

Now, choose an extract from any textbook you use and reduce it to note form using the ideas here.

Section 5

MAKING PRESENTATIONS

Teachers' notes
- 5.1 What makes a good presentation?
- 5.2 Planning a presentation
- 5.5 Preparing what to say
- 5.8 Using body language
- 5.10 Using visual aids

Teachers' notes
MAKING PRESENTATIONS

Many students find making oral presentations extremely frightening. This section aims to reduce that anxiety by encouraging careful thought, planning and organisation.

What makes a good presentation? The first activity aims to help students identify some of the factors that make presentations more or less successful. As an extension activity students could identify different types of presentation and discuss what 'giving a presentation' actually means. Ideas may be offered such as, *telling others about something they have done or something that has happened, presenting findings of a project or experiment, reporting back from work experience.*

Planning a presentation and **Preparing what to say** encourage consideration of the setting of the presentation as well as its audience, purpose and planning. Make sure students are aware that people make judgements based on both *what* is said and *how* it is said and that the presenter must be clear about what exactly it is they are trying to achieve. Students could benefit from watching a presentation of the *News* on TV, paying particular attention to the structure of the broadcast - the introduction, the main part of the presentation and the closing. Follow this up by discussing that, typically, a presentation comprises of a beginning (20%), middle (60%) and an end (20%).

The activities can also be used as a basis to look at language use and audience appropriateness. Collect some topics for presentations, for example, *Banning homework, The closing down of a local factory, The truth about Father Christmas.* Ask students to identify a wide range of audiences such as *under fives, war veterans, allergy sufferers* and so on. Then assess the appropriateness of the chosen topics for each of the audiences suggested. Students could then work in pairs giving one chosen talk, first to an appropriate audience, then to an inappropriate one; for example, *Banning homework* to war veterans and school children. Follow up the activity with discussion concerning appropriate register and the need for clear objectives.

Using body language. The best way to learn about body language is to become aware of it in both ourselves and in others through practical activities. Role playing 'negative' body language is an unthreatening way for students to understand what not to do. Use simple topics such as *My journey to school/college, A proud moment* or *My first bike.* Ask students to talk for two or three minutes having chosen one or two roles and non-verbal behaviours from these lists: *sad, nervous, threatening, bored. Cough regularly, fidget with your collar, look out of the window a lot, stand without moving your arms or legs at all, avoid eye contact.* The list can be extended. At the end of the talk the audience can try to identify the negative behaviour and discuss its likely effect on an audience. Discuss how standing behind a desk, 'hiding' behind notes and avoiding eye contact, creates barriers. Students can be advised that, for small group audiences, the presenter should look at eye level. In larger groups eye contact is achieved more successfully by using an 'M' shaped eye movement, as this will encompass everyone.

Using visual aids. Students might be asked why most presentations use visual aids. Their answers may include: *to actively involve the audience, to act as a prompt for the speaker, to add colour or humour, to lodge key points in the audiences mind and to give the audience the chance to use their eyes as well as their ears.* It is also useful to collect ideas regarding the disadvantages of using a visual aid. For example, if the presenter depends on an OHP they could be in a difficult position if it broke down - the audience may stop listening and use the aid as a chance to be distracted. Emphasise the point that, to be effective, the visual must add to the impact of the talk.

MAKING PRESENTATIONS   Section 5 – 1

WHAT MAKES A GOOD PRESENTATION?

You are likely to be something of an expert at presentations. After all, you've experienced many hundreds as a school pupil. What factors make them interesting, lively and educational or boring, dull and useless? If you can work this out then you're well on the way to making your own successful presentations.

How important is the advice in this table?

When making a presentation you should:	Very important for success	Quite important	To be avoided
Use short sentences			
Use long words wherever possible			
Read from a script			
Avoid looking at the audience			
Keep smiling			
Stand behind a desk			
Write notes on separate cards			
Wave your arms around to emphasise points			
Keep talking whatever happens			
Make it clear you know best			
Use at least five visual aids			
Encourage questioning			
Move around as much as possible			
Plan the presentation carefully			
Have a few jokes ready			

Write down two other presentation skills that are very important for success and two more to be avoided.

Important for success

1. _____

2. _____

To be avoided

1. _____

2. _____

Finally, think of a talk or presentation that you have listened to that was successful. Write a paragraph explaining why you considered it a success.

© CONNECT Publications 1999

PLANNING A PRESENTATION

Successful presentations are carefully planned. Presenters need to consider a variety of factors when planning:

- the setting of the presentation
- the audience for the presentation
- the purpose of the presentation

Let's look at each of these in turn.

The setting of the presentation

The way a room is arranged can make a significant difference to the success of a presentation.

Think of a classroom containing 15 desks and chairs, a teacher's desk and a teacher's chair. Draw plans to show how you could best arrange the desks and chairs in order to:

1. To stimulate discussion

2. Discourage discussion

3. Give a presentation

The audience for the presentation

People are very different so different things interest and motivate them. For some football is fascinating, for others it is a total 'turn off'. Presenters need to think carefully about their audiences and adjust their language and style to suit different groups of people.

Imagine making a successful presentation to a group of eight year old children about something they really weren't very interested in. Then giving a talk about the same subject to a group of highly motivated adults. The language and style of presentation ought to be very different.

We need to know as much as possible about our audience. If we can find out about factors like their age, educational ability, gender, interests, race and so on then we can adjust our language and approach to suit those particular people.

Choose *one* of these topics:

Pensions	War memorials	The price of CD's
Line dancing	Horse riding	Taking up hairdressing
Protecting dolphins	The importance of university education	

Choose *two* sets of audiences suitable for the topic. Ring round your choices.

7 - 8 year olds	News presenters	Teachers
Retired people	Physically challenged	Royalty
University students		

How would your language and approach for each audience of the presentation differ?

Audience 1

Audience 2

If you can, compare your plans with another student. How did you take into account the differences between the audiences?

If you have the opportunity, give a 'mock' talk on either of the topics. Ask fellow students to guess who your audience is.

MAKING PRESENTATIONS   Section 5 – 4

The purpose of the presentation

Every presentation has a purpose. Perhaps the aim is to encourage certain types of behaviour, change attitudes or raise awareness of something. Perhaps the aim is simply to entertain the audience. Whatever the aim, presenters need to be clear about what exactly their presentation hopes to achieve and how they can check whether that aim has been achieved.

A good way of focusing clearly on purpose is to set **SMART** objectives.
SMART stands for:

Specific   –   be clear about the intended outcomes
Measurable   –   will you know if you have achieved what you set out to do? How?
Appropriate   –   suitable for your audience
Realistic   –   achievable
Time bonded   –   what is the time limit in which your objectives should have been achieved?

Using the SMART approach, judge the likely effectiveness of the aims of the presentations below. The first has been done for you.

Audience	Purpose	S Specific	M Measurable	A Appropriate	R Realistic	T Time-bonded
1. Old age pensioners	To persuade them to take up skate boarding by June	✓	✓	✗	✗	✓
2. College friends	To encourage them not to drop litter					
3. Parents	To educate them about illegal drugs.					
4. Young children	To persuade them to clean their teeth after every meal					

How could the success of each of the above presentations be judged?

1. _____
   _____
2. _____
   _____
3. _____
   _____
4. _____
   _____

© **CONNECT** Publications 1999

PREPARING WHAT TO SAY

Giving a talk is pretty scary at the best of times. But what if you forgot some of the points that you wanted to make or made all of them quickly at the beginning and then ran out of things to say? Worst of all, what if you just dried up and were completely lost for words?

All of these terrors can be avoided with a little planning and preparation. You need to work out:

- the areas to be covered
- the research needed
- the method of making notes for the talk
- the structure and organisation of the talk.

Let's look at each of these in turn by using an example. Imagine you were given the task of giving a five minute talk with the title *Cruelty to animals*.

The areas to be covered
Here are three sub-headings for your talk: *Vivisection, Animal experimentation* and *Circus animals*. Think of three other sub-headings that might be included.

1. _____
2. _____
3. _____

Research
Ask yourself some basic questions.
- What do I already know?
- What else do I need to know?
- Where will I go to find this out?

Read through the areas you're going to cover and identify what you need to find out more about.

Things I need to find out	Where I can get the information from
e.g. RSPCA's view	e.g. write to RSPCA

Making notes for the talk
The first stage is to make your own notes on each of the areas you've decided to cover. Then condense the information into a series of key points. Now you can copy each collection of key points onto separate 'nudge' cards (called this as their aim is to *nudge* your memory).

MAKING PRESENTATIONS   Section 5 – 6

Here are some *nudge* cards for your presentation on *Cruelty to animals*. Fill in three more bullet points for each card.

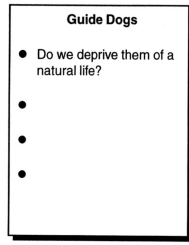
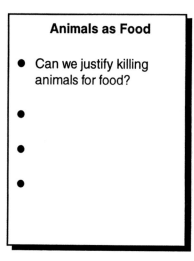

Experiments
- Should we use animals for testing drugs?
- Should we use them for testing make-up?
-
-
-

Guide Dogs
- Do we deprive them of a natural life?
-
-
-

Animals as Food
- Can we justify killing animals for food?
-
-
-

The structure and organisation of the talk

However thorough the information collected, your presentation will make little sense unless the material is organised in such a way that one point follows on from another.

Once all the information is collected and condensed it's time to think about the best order to put it in.

Look at the areas you have already identified. In which order would you use the *nudge* cards in your presentation? Number the cards and explain why you chose that order.

Now look at the *cards* above once again. Think about the key points and number each in the order you would present them.

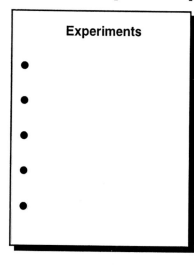
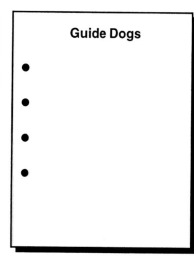
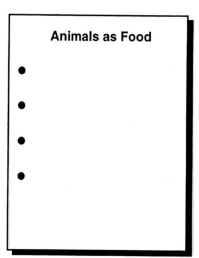

Experiments
-
-
-
-
-

Guide Dogs
-
-
-
-

Animals as Food
-
-
-
-

© **CONNECT** Publications 1999

MAKING PRESENTATIONS   Section 5 – 7

On the cards below write an *Introduction* and *Summary* to your talk. Some useful phrases are provided.

Introduction
- The purpose of this talk ....
- I am here to discuss ....
- 'Cruelty to animals'. What is cruelty?
- I am going to raise some questions concerning ....
- I am particularly interested in ....

Introduction

Summary
- Finally, ...
- In conclusion, ...
- To sum up, ...
- As we have seen, ...
- I have raised many points ....

Summary

Keep your cards at hand to refer to during the presentation, turning them over as you finish with them.

Here are some other useful phrases to use in your talk:

'On the other hand', 'although some may argue', 'research has shown', 'as we all know', 'contrary to popular belief', 'in my opinion', 'have you ever thought about', 'I'm sure you will agree'.

Collect some more by listening to presentations on TV and radio.

Finally, try your talk out on a friend or fellow student. Time it. Is it long enough? Do you need more information? Make a list of any audio/visual aids you could use in order to support and add variety to the talk.

© CONNECT Publications 1999

USING BODY LANGUAGE

When we give a talk or presentation we are not just judged on *what* we say but on *how* we say it. Enthusiasm and interest are created by variation in the way presenters speak and move.

We can tell a great deal about people through their body language. Look around – you will find some people 'walking tall' and obviously feeling good about themselves. Others might be 'creeping around', shoulders and head down.

Try watching a TV programme with the sound turned off. See what you can tell from the body language.

Look at how people enter a room, where they sit, how they sit or stand. Do they make eye contact? Each body is giving out what are called non-verbal messages.

Read this story and underline all the body language references.

> Tom walked in and sat quietly in the corner. He avoided looking at his parents. He would know soon enough if they had the note from college or not. His mother glanced at him and nodded towards his father who was standing with his back to them, apparently looking out of the window.
>
> Tom crossed his legs and strummed his fingers on the armchair. His mother leaned forward and frowned. Tom stopped and sprawled back, looking at the ceiling. His father had a piece of paper in one hand which he tapped with the other. Tom pulled the cushion from behind his head and put it on his lap as he pulled both feet up on the chair. His mother frowned – he took his feet down.
>
> Tom's father turned round and stared into Tom's eyes. Tom quickly looked away. His mother stood up and linked arms with Tom's father, they both looked at him. Tom folded, then unfolded his arms. 'Well' said his father, 'I got the job!'. 'So this isn't about college,' thought Tom. He stood up, smiling. He shook his dad's hands and patted him on the shoulder. He was temporarily reprieved....

Write **P** next to each positive signal and **N** next to each negative signal.

Think of five words which could describe Tom e.g. *nervous*.

1. _____   2. _____
3. _____   4. _____
5. _____

Imagine you are making a presentation. Which of these behaviours would be likely to have a positive effect on the audience and which negative. Put a **P** or **N** after each statement.

- Keeping your eyes on the floor.
- Smiling.

- Keeping your hands in your pockets.
- Maintaining eye contact.
- Staring out of the window from time to time.
- Keeping your arms crossed as you talk.
- Emphasising points with your hands.
- Leaning forward to answer a question.

Finally list five more presentation body language 'do's' and five presentation body language 'don'ts'.

Do	**Don't**
1.	1.
2.	2.
3.	3.
4.	4.
5.	5.

MAKING PRESENTATIONS   Section 5 – 10

USING VISUAL AIDS

Visual aids can bring variety and clarity to a presentation. But they do need to be used well.

Here is a list of some of the more common visual aids.

- Flip Charts
- Overhead projector
- Slides
- Video

Which of the following statements about the use of visual aids are true and which false?

A good presenter will:	True	False
Make sure everyone can see the visual		
Not worry if everyone can't see it		
Use lots of different visuals		
Be prepared if the equipment fails		
Not need a trial run before using the visual		
Talk to the visual, not the audience		
Talk and show visuals at the same time		
Never use cartoons to emphasise a point		
Use colour where possible		
Plan at what stage of the talk the visuals will be used		

Three students are making presentations. Each intends to use a different visual aid or combination of visual aids. Help each one by identifying five things to remember to do before the presentation. The first has been done for you.

Sara is using a video.

1. *Check that a video player is available.*

2. _____

3. _____

4. _____

5. _____

© CONNECT Publications 1999

MAKING PRESENTATIONS

Tom is planning to use a flip chart

1. _____
2. _____
3. _____
4. _____
5. _____

.... and slides

1. _____
2. _____
3. _____
4. _____
5. _____

Sam is using an OHP (overhead projector)

1. _____
2. _____
3. _____
4. _____
5. _____

Next, read this written OHT (overhead transparency) message:

> I'm sickened by the rising tide of filth on our beaches. I suggest we launch a nationwide clear up campaign to rid us of sewage in the water, litter – including broken glass – on the beach, dead fish washed up on the shore and oil that ruins your clothes when you're sitting on the beach.

Now design an OHT that gets this same message across but by using illustration rather than text. Use the tee shirt test to assess it. That is, there should be no more words on an OHT than you would be able to read on someone's tee shirt.

Now, take some tips about what not to do from the 'THIMBLE' list.

- Do not **T**alk to the visual aid – talk to the audience.
- Do not **H**urry it away before the audience has had time to look at it.
- Do not **I**gnore it – we don't want to have to guess why it's there.
- Do not **M**ove it about all the time.
- Do not **B**lock its view.
- Do not **L**eave it there too long.
- Do not **E**xamine it in detail – just let the audience extract their own understanding.

Section 6

WRITING AT LENGTH: ESSAYS, SPELLING AND PUNCTUATION

Teachers' notes
- 6.1 Decoding essay titles
- 6.3 Planning essays
- 6.5 Paragraphs
- 6.7 Connecting phrases and sentences
- 6.8 Introductions and conclusions
- 6.10 Spell well
- 6.13 Improving punctuation

Teachers' notes
WRITING AT LENGTH: ESSAYS, SPELLING AND PUNCTUATION

This section deals with the problems posed by essays and all longer pieces of writing. It includes the technical problems of spelling and punctuation.

Decoding essay titles explains why it is necessary to pick essay titles to pieces in order to get to the central question. Students could write their own definitions for the following key words and compare their answers with a partner: *analyse, account for, compare, contrast, critically evaluate, define, describe, distinguish, discuss, explain, illustrate, justify, outline, summarise, trace*. Encourage the use of a dictionary for definition checking.

The **Planning essays** activity is designed to encourage students to see the importance of structuring essays before writing them. A useful extension activity is to further consider the different ways in which a paragraph may be developed. Ask students in what contexts the following may be used: *chronological order* (to narrate the plot of a novel, sum up the highlights of a particular event, explain how an artist created a sculpture); *spatial order* (to describe the setting and structure of a building, the solar system, the set of a play); *descending order* (to explain how best to prepare for an examination, the way a child plays with toys, an organisation's administrative structure); *climactic order* (to describe the events leading to Macbeth's downfall, style changes in cars over the years, a child opening Christmas presents); *cause and effect* (to describe the conditions that led to World War Two, the effects of a misunderstanding, the behavioural effects of negligence on a child); *comparison and contrast* (to compare sonnets, different democracies, different types of family); *definition* (to explain the concept of morality, the component parts of an electron, the categorisation of animals or people in society).

Paragraphs is an activity designed to raise awareness of the importance of *paragraph flow*. As a follow-up, students could write a paragraph with one deliberate mistake (a sentence unrelated to the main idea). A partner can read to pick this 'odd one out'.

Connecting Phrases and Sentences. A very useful whole class extension activity is to ask students to categorise each linking phrase from the list in the activity under the following headings: *addition, sequence, contrast, comparison, result, time, place, summation, example, intensity, repetition*. Students could also collect together some ideas for paragraph starters that would be useful in their particular subjects. Having a 'good ideas' list of *linkers* and *starters* is very reassuring to those who find their work lacks that necessary *flow*.

The purpose of the activity **Introductions and conclusions** is to help students 'cocoon' their ideas within a coherent framework by neatly opening and closing the 'curtains' of the essay. By taking any one recent essay title a whole group or class could discuss how they interpret the question, what issues they intend to cover and in what order they intend to deal with those issues. Students find it very useful to read concluding paragraphs from subject texts and discuss how the main points of the text have been summarised and conclusions reached. Ask them to 'predict' the contents of the main body of a chapter by reading the summary/conclusion only.

The Spell well activity is designed to improve spelling by adopting a problem solving approach. In order to retain words in the long term students need to *need* the words and thus understand the importance of being able to spell them correctly. They also need to 'overlearn' difficult words that stubbornly refuse to go into the long term memory. Ten ways of achieving this are suggested. Invite students to suggest other ways and to discuss the methods that work for them. Sharing ideas is important. Many students, even at the 16 plus stage of education, benefit from *word lists* containing new vocabulary or commonly misspelt subject related words that can be placed on a classroom wall or printed sheet.

The **Improving punctuation** activity is designed to make students more *punctuation aware*. As an extension activity students might write a narrative, report or essay introduction deliberately leaving out any punctuation. They can then exchange this with a partner who will correct the work for punctuation. Students can then discuss the accuracy of the marking.

DECODING ESSAY TITLES

Every essay title is a problem to be solved. To solve any problem you must first understand the exact nature of that problem. In the case of essays this means understanding – or decoding – the question.

Examiners' instructions

Essay titles include one or more words that give you exact instructions as to what the examiner is looking for. These are typically words like *discuss* and *examine*. They indicate what skills you need to demonstrate in order to answer the question successfully. Essays usually test one or more of the following skills.

1. Your knowledge and understanding.
2. Your ability to interpret or work out the reasons for something.
3. Your ability to evaluate, make judgements and assess the value of different ideas.
4. A mixture of the above.

Which of the above skills or combinations of skills are required by the following examiners' instructions?

	1	2	3	4
Describe				
Analyse				
Define				
Assess				
To what extent				
Outline				
Discuss				
Compare				
Contrast				
Examine				

Decoding the question

Once you know what skills are needed you can move on to look at the question as a whole and begin to *decode* it.

Let's look at an example of this 'decoding' process in action.

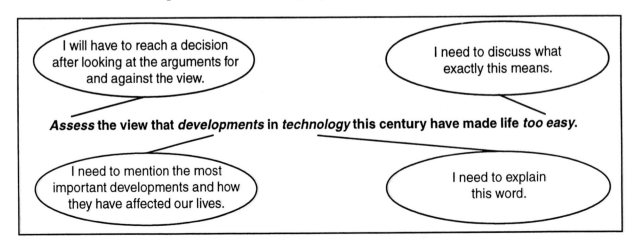

Now try it yourself with the following title.

To what extent do you agree that terrorism can never be justified?

Once you've worked out what the question is about you can begin to identify what exactly your answer will need to include. Let's take our first example. From our analysis of the question we can work out these *'I must'* statements.

To answer this question:

I must	explain the word *technology*.
I must	discuss what *too easy* actually means.
I must	identify key developments in technology this century and explain how they have affected our lives.
I must	discuss the arguments for and against this view.
I must	reach my own decision on the merits of these arguments

Try and work out some *'I must'* statements from your own analysis of the title above.

To answer this question:

I must _____

I must _____

I must _____

I must _____

I must _____

Now you can take some essay titles from any subject you study and try to *decode* the questions using the ideas here.

PLANNING ESSAYS

Many essay writers take a quick look at the title and begin to write. They're understandably concerned about getting all the information down in a short space of time. Unfortunately they are not likely to achieve a high mark.

Think of two reasons why this approach is not likely to be effective.

1. _____

2. _____

So how do you go about planning what to write?

The first stage is to generate the ideas, then to put them into a sensible order.

Generating ideas

It's useful to 'brainstorm' the key words and phrases in the question so you get lots of possible ideas for inclusion in the essay.

Imagine an essay title: *Discuss the relationship between people and animals.*

A 'brainstorm' on this title has been started. Add some ideas of your own.

```
Farming   Guide dogs   Hunting   Vets   Working animals   Pets

Vegetarians — Discuss the relationship between people and animals — Zoos

Circus animals   RSPCA   Animal liberation   CJD/BSE   Police dogs
```

Add three more ideas of your own

1. _____ 2. _____ 3. _____

Organising ideas

Once you have a list of possible content you can begin to think about organising your ideas into the most effective order.

Try to find links between the ideas above. Divide some of the ideas into different sections. One has been done for you as an example.

Possible sections	
Section title	*Use of animals for pleasure*
Content	*Circus animals, zoos, hunting, pets*
Section title	_____
Content	_____
Section title	_____
Content	_____
Section title	_____
Content	_____

What order might these sections go in to create the best 'flow' of ideas?

Best order of sections and reasons for choice

Can you see how, by ordering ideas into sections that each contain one main idea and then planning the order of those sections, your essays will *flow*?

Essay structure

The actual plan or structure that you use for an essay will depend on the title. However, there are some structures that are quite common and can be used 'off the peg'.

1. Arguments and evidence in favour of something followed by arguments against (or vice versa).
2. Listing a series of points in order of importance (most important can be first or last).
3. Listing a series of events in the order they occurred (chronological order).
4. Going through the causes of something followed by their effects.
5. Listing similarities followed by differences.

From the list above, choose the structure that best fits the following essay titles.

	Best structure (*use number above*)
a. Compare and contrast writing an essay with writing in note form.	
b. What factors should be borne in mind when revising for exams?	
c. What reasons can be given for the existence of violence in societies?	
d. 'Abortion is murder'. Discuss this statement.	
e. Describe the process which leads to rainfall.	

Now choose three essay titles from the subjects you study and try to plan answers.

PARAGRAPHS

Have you ever been told that your essays do not 'flow' or that you need to improve the 'structure' of your writing? These sorts of comments are particularly annoying when you feel confident that you know a lot but lose marks simply because you aren't able to organise what you know into a logical framework. The key to improving this aspect of your writing lies in understanding **paragraphs**.

A paragraph is a group of sentences which all relate to a particular theme. To find out a bit more about their key features let's look at an example.

The overall theme of this paragraph is that babies are learning all the time.

> *The first sentence describes the theme of the paragraph.*
>
> Babies are learning and developing all the time. They learn to recognise the face, the feel, the taste, the smell and the sound of the mother from the moment they are born. Touching and feeling objects helps them begin to understand where their bodies end and the rest of the world begins. Every contact with another person teaches them how their different actions provoke different responses.
>
> *The other sentences contribute to the development of the theme by giving examples and/or developing ideas and arguments.*

Right. Now it's your turn. Here is a series of sentences that have been written as part of an essay entitled: *Discuss the arguments for and against the replacement of student grants by loans.* The problem is that they're not in a logical order. Re-arrange them in the box below so they make up a coherent paragraph.

1. Students from families on lower incomes may be especially put off applying to college because financial support from parents is less likely.
2. Although loans are given at low interest students leaving university will still be faced with significant debt at a time when many need money for other purposes such as setting up a family and home.
3. Evidence from UCAS shows that there was an 8% drop in applications in 1998.
4. One of the most important arguments against the replacement of grants by loans is that loans will discourage participation in higher education.
5. Potential students will be discouraged from applying for higher education because they do not want to face debt at the end of their studies.

Once you've got the basic idea of a paragraph you should be able to build up your own. Let's take a pretty straightforward essay title: *Discuss the problems caused by extreme weather.*

First, think of five themes or main ideas the essay might include, for example, *The problem of homelessness.*

Choose one of these themes or main ideas.

List some ideas and examples that could develop this theme.

Now write a paragraph about this theme on a sheet of paper.

- Underline the main idea.
- Tick each sentence that develops the main idea.
- Underline the final sentence.
- Tick it if it 'flags' the way to the next main idea.
- Rewrite the paragraph if necessary until you have kept it to these 'rules'.

Finally, select a paragraph from a text book you use.

How easy is it to find the main theme of the paragraph? (*circle the appropriate number*).

Very easy   1   2   3   4   5   Very hard

And how well does the rest of the paragraph develop the theme?

Very well   1   2   3   4   5   Not well at all

Good essay planning really helps you to construct good paragraphs. Planning an essay involves identifying its main themes and working out the best order in which to put them. Each theme usually consists of one paragraph. So, by planning the essay, you are actually working out what each paragraph will include.

CONNECTING PHRASES AND SENTENCES

Good writing always seems to 'flow'. One point or idea links almost effortlessly with the next. How is this achieved?

An important technique is the use of words and phrases whose job it is to link, or connect, sentences and phrases.

Here is a list of linking phrases.

> in addition, evidence to support this can be found in, in the first place, moreover, an illustration of this is, furthermore, besides, likewise, finally, lastly, and, too, on the other hand, against this it could be argued, however, on the contrary, but, nevertheless, similarly, therefore, accordingly, consequently, thus, meanwhile, in the meantime, afterwards, soon, then, nearby, opposite to, beyond, here, to sum up, all in all, on the whole, on balance, it could be claimed, as a consequence of this, in conclusion, for example, for instance, such as, in fact, indeed, as I have pointed out, in other words, that is.

Underline ten linking phrases that could be used to continue this sentence (there are more if you wish to find them).

Individual talents are important . . . .

(For example 'Individual talents are important, <u>therefore</u>...')

OK, now ring round ten different *linkers* that could continue this sentence:

Humans will pollute themselves out of existence . . . .

Can you see how linking phrases help sentence and paragraph *'flow'*? They are an important part of writing essays and remind you to develop, qualify and provide examples for, the points you make.

Next, make up a sentence for each of the linking words and phrases that are not marked above. Write them on a sheet of paper.

Finally, take a textbook from one of your subject areas and find five linking phrases.

Write the words or phrases here.

1. _____
2. _____
3. _____
4. _____
5. _____

Why not note down the *linkers* above to refer to when you are writing essays?

INTRODUCTIONS AND CONCLUSIONS

We are often told that our essays should have introductions and conclusions but what exactly are they and what should they contain?

Introductions

The introduction to an essay will refer to the essay title and talk about the topic in general terms, giving a broad 'lead-in' to what is to be discussed in the essay.

The introductory paragraph gives you the chance to:

1. Define and limit the scope of the essay.
2. Outline the proposed methods of development of the essay.
3. Set the overall mood and dominant attitude of the essay. In fact the introduction serves as a preview of what is to come and a preview should be fairly brief, simply offering an indication of what is to come and tempting the reader to want to know more.

How does the following paragraph satisfy these three requirements of a good introduction?

> This essay attempts to tackle the basic problems of one parent families through discussing the financial problems the single parent encounters. It demonstrates how financial restraints affect educational and job opportunities in the short term and the quality of living in the long term.

Tick or cross as appropriate.   1. _ _ _ _ _ _ _ 2. _ _ _ _ _ _ _ 3. _ _ _ _ _ _ _

Now, these introductory paragraphs are poorly written. Rewrite them using the tips above.

> 1. I don't agree that children need to start school by the age of five. In some countries they start at six and they are not behind as adults. I think socialising at a young age is most important.
>
> 2. Home based workstations are becoming necessary in our computerised world. Think of the time saved in travelling, the fares saved and the stress. Throw out the briefcase and bring in the home based workstation, communicate by screen and leave more time for leisure.
>
> 3. When King Claudius in Hamlet (Act IV scene v) says that sorrows come not as single 'spies' but as 'battalions' he means that a lot of sorrowful events have come at once. The audience is also made aware that more sorrowful events are yet to come.

Finally, look through one of your subject texts and choose an introductory paragraph. How effective is it at giving you a preview of what is to come?

Conclusions

A concluding paragraph gives a lasting impression. It should be brief - no longer that a tenth of the essay - but is powerful as it is the last thing the marker reads. A conclusion serves a number of purpose. It enables you to:

1. Refer back to the central question raised in the title.
2. Restate the main ideas that the essay has developed.
3. Summarise your main points and show how they relate to each other.
4. Draw general conclusions.
5. Comment on the significance of those conclusions.

What it must *not* do is:

1. 'Go off' in a new direction.
2. Throw in any comments that are not related to the title.
3. Express any new ideas.

Does this paragraph meet the requirements of a good conclusion?

> Morality, then, seems to be concerned with three things. Firstly with fair play and harmony between individuals. Secondly with what might be called tidying up or harmonising the things inside each individual. Thirdly, with the general purpose of human life as a whole; what man was made for; what course the whole fleet ought to be on; what tune the conductor of the band wants it to play. (*C.S.Lewis, Mere Christianity, Fount 1997*)

- If the above had been the conclusion to an essay, what do you think the title might have been?
- On a separate sheet of paper, write an introduction for the same essay title.
- What do you think the first main paragraph would have been about?
- The second?
- The third?

Can you see how much you can tell about an essay simply from reading a good concluding paragraph?

Remember, the conclusion is the final chance to make an impression on the reader.

Now, read two concluding paragraphs, each from a different subject textbook. How effective are they?

Finally, select two of your recent essays and read your final paragraphs. How could you improve them? Rewrite one of them as an example of an 'ideal' conclusion.

SPELL WELL

Here is a list of 100 common spelling troublemakers.

abseil	equipment	muscular	sincerely
accessories	equipped	necessary	skilful
accident	exaggerate	noticeable	success
accommodation	exercise	occasion	suffragette
acquiring	fibre	occurred	summary
addictive	foreign	omitted	sustenance
address	focused	omniscient	technique
aesthetic	fulfil	onomatopoeia	temperament
aggressive	gauge	parallel	temporary
analysis	government	patriarchal	territory
benefited	guarantee	precede	therapeutic
breathalyser	illegible	programmed	twelfth
business	illusive	pronunciation	ultimatum
changeable	incandescent	psychologist	utilitarianism
chargeable	inconspicuous	qualitative	vacuum
committed	irresponsible	quantitative	variance
conscience	itinerary	quark	vein
cosmonaut	judiciary	questionnaire	vengeance
crystallise	juxtaposition	receive	vicissitude
deceive	leisure	recommend	voluminous
deferred	library	referee	warrior
deviance	lyric	referred	wrench
disseminate	maintenance	regrettable	yields
dyslexia	meritocracy	scenario	yolk
embarrass	miscellaneous	separate	zealot

Work with a partner if you can. Highlight five words from the list above. Ask them to do the same. Then cover up the list and test each other. Now analyse any errors taking one word at a time.

Word _

- Did you get the right letters but in the wrong order?
- Did you miss out any letters?
- Did you get just the ending wrong?
- Did you get it wrong in another way? If so, explain the error in one sentence below.

_ _

- Did you get it right? If so, write a sentence here explaining to someone who got it wrong, what might be a good way to remember that word next time.

_ _

Repeat the exercise until you have analysed all five words.

Target words

Think of three words from the subjects you study that challenge your spelling power. Look through past work if necessary.

1. _____ 2. _____ 3. _____

These are your target words for the week. You are going put them in your long term memory by taking these ten steps.

1. Write the word first with your eyes open, then with your eyes closed (yes, I mean it), saying each letter as you write it (e.g. 'therapeutic, therapeutic').
2. (Open your eyes!) Now write it again but this time write the letters that cause problems in a bright colour (thera**peu**tic).
3. Now break the word into syllables and write each syllable in a different colour (the rap eu tic).
4. See if you can attach a mnemonic to the part that causes problems (**a**ll **p**ain **e**ases **u**p = apeu) or look for smaller words within that word that will help you remember it (*the rap* eu *tic*).
5. Say the words above - the sillier the sounds the more likely you are to remember!
6. Count how many letters are in the word. (Therapeutic = 11. Think of 11 therapuetic sessions.)
7. Think of a similar word to start a 'word family' (therapy, therapist).
8. Write each letter on separate tiny 'post-its' or scraps of paper and see how quickly you can 'make' the word.
9. Write the word out in one bright colour. Look at it for eight seconds then close your eyes and 'see' it written on someone's tee shirt.
10. Write it on a 'post-it' and take it home. Stick the 'post-it' on your mirror so you look at it each time you look in the mirror. (How many times you look at it will depend on how often you admire yourself in the mirror!)

Don't forget to add at least one word a week to the list.

The most common cause of spelling errors are:
- word endings
- words containing double letters
- words containing *ie* or *ei*
- words which sound alike but which are spelt differently, for example *aloud* and *allowed*. These words are called homophones.

Let's look at two of these in more detail, homophones and word endings.

Homophones

Here is a list of some homophones.

• weather (*hot, cold, rainy*)	whether (*if*)
• aloud (*not silently*)	allowed (*with permission*)
• their (*belonging to someone*)	there (*in that place*)
• past (*not the present*)	passed (*passed by*)

© **CONNECT** Publications 1999

How could we help someone who mixed up these word pairs? Here are three examples.

1. The **weather** with the '*ea*' in it could remind us of **e**arly **a**utumn and the **whether** with '**he**' in it would be in the sentence, '*I don't know whether **he** would want to come*'.
2. **Aloud** as in s**hout** and **allowed** as in *to* **wed** (given permission).
3. **Their**, as in the **heir** to the throne, is a person and **there**, with **here** in it, means a place.

Now you try with these three homophones.

- sight (*something seen*) site (*a location like a building site*)
- principle (*a personal standard*) principal (*the one in charge*)
- its (*of it*) it's (*abbreviated form of it is*)

Next, think of five more homophones (work with a partner if you can).

1. _____
2. _____
3. _____
4. _____
5. _____

Refer to a dictionary if you need to. Identify the meanings and work out some tips to help remember them.

Word endings

Can you work out why the letters in these words double when a suffix (a word ending) is added?

begin	beginning
regret	regretting
fit	fitting
permit	permitting

But why does *focus* become *focusing* and not *focussing*?

Why do you think these words do *not* double the final letter when a word ending is added?

dine	dining
wave	waving
believe	believing
focus	focusing

Working out rules needs a problem solving approach and can be a rewarding process. Unfortunately there are always some words that break the rules and these are best learnt by memory.

IMPROVING PUNCTUATION

Does the word 'punctuation' fill you with dread?
Well, by knowing the basic rules you will soon become a lot more confident.

Read this passage. It contains all the basic punctuation. Each sentence has been numbered.

> On the wall was his secretary's notice: "Monday 17th July, the following members won awards this month: Mr. Rhani, Miss Tiler, E.M. Short."(1) He looked in the drawer. (2) It contained pens, pencils, paper clips and the notebook. (3) His idea was a brilliant one; it would show the others that he meant business. (4) He had decided that the exhibition would be held in Holland and would include children, old people and the physically challenged. (5) He picked up his secretary's notebook, checked that no one could see him, and sat down. (6) The notebook was covered with pictures of women's coats and children's smiling faces and there was a sketch of a dog with its tongue hanging out. (7) Inside there were details of the representatives' calls, the secretaries' meeting times and the books' prices. (8) He put it down (he would read it later) and looked at the clock. (9) She came in carrying a copy of "Jude The Obscure" by Thomas Hardy. (10)
> "What are you doing Dr. James?" she asked. (11) He smiled and asked if she wanted a coffee. (12)
> "It's incredible!" she said, "you always manage to avoid the question". (13)
> "I don't," he smiled, "I came to ask you to make a note that the exhibition will include the young, the old, the disabled and 'down and outs'." (14)

Read sentence (1). Highlight the punctuation.

Now, go through all 14 sentences and tick the appropriate boxes below. Sentence 1 has been done for you.

	1	2	3	4	5	6	7	8	9	10	11	12	13	14
Capital letter	✓													
Full stop	✓													
Comma	✓													
Semi-colon														
Colon	✓													
Apostrophe	✓													
Bracket														
Question mark														
Exclamation mark														
Quotation marks	✓													

Next, fill in the missing words in the following definitions of punctuation marks. The first has been done for you.

1. A *capital letter* begins each sentence and is used for names of people and places, days of the week and months of the year.

2. A _ _ _ _ _ _ _ _ shows the end of the sentence, also that a word has been abbreviated.

3. A _ _ _ _ _ _ _ _ is used within sentences to indicate a pause between groups of words, also to separate words.
4. A _ _ _ _ _ _ _ _ allows for a dramatic pause – somewhere between a comma and a full stop. It gives added impact to the words that follow it.
5. A _ _ _ _ _ _ _ _ introduces an example or quotation.
6. An _ _ _ _ _ _ _ _ denotes possession or indicates that a letter or letters have been left out of a word.
7. _ _ _ _ _ _ _ _ are used to separate what is often a secondary or additional idea from the rest of the sentence.
8. The _ _ _ _ _ _ _ _ is placed at the end of direct questions and inside any quotation marks.
9. The _ _ _ _ _ _ _ _ is used to indicate surprise, astonishment, sarcasm or enthusiasm.
10. _ _ _ _ _ _ _ _ _ _ are placed around direct quotations (speech), also around the title of a story, article, poem, book and so on.

Find examples from the passage of each of these ten punctuation marks.

Now we can focus on some of the more common difficulties faced in punctuation.

- Look at sentences 7 and 13. When do we use *it's* and when do we use *its*?
- Look at sentence 11. Where does the question mark come, inside or outside the quotation marks?
- Look at sentences 7 and 8. Why does the apostrophe showing ownership come before the *s* at some times and after the *s* at other times?
- Look at the word *secretary's* in sentence one and *secretaries'* in sentence 8. Explain the different use of the apostrophe.

Finally, write a short story using as much of the punctuation above as you can.

Section 7

DEALING WITH STRESS

Teachers' notes
- 7.1 Recognising and dealing with stress
- 7.4 Stress and time management
- 7.5 Exams and stress

Teachers' notes
DEALING WITH STRESS

Most students experience stress at some time. Its source may be study related or may derive from outside sources and impact on their studies. Either way it is an issue that needs to be addressed.

Recognising and dealing with stress. This activity helps students to become aware of, and take responsibility for, their feelings. By breaking the cycle of negative reactions to stress (panic) using a CALM approach students will become aware of the importance of a problem solving approach to dealing with stress. As an extension activity students could discuss how stress is a necessary part of life in that it can lead to personal growth and ensure that necessary life-coping skills are learned. By providing an opportunity to discuss and compare their different stress related experiences and responses students will see that each individual needs to find the optimum level that is right for them. Students may wish to consider their reactions to situations that have too few demands (*boredom, lack of motivation*) and too many demands (*anxiety, panic, fatigue, confusion, 'burn out'*) as well as 'ideal' demands (*challenging, motivating, rewarding*). They could draw a 'stress curve' using all the collected 'reactions' before deciding where 'peak performance' would come.

By considering their reactions to study related situations e.g. *'I am motivated when a deadline is near'*, *'I panic when I don't plan'*, students can see how a great deal of study related stress and 'burnout' (physical, emotional and mental exhaustion occurring as a result of long term involvement in study habits that are not effective) can be avoided.

Stress and time management reminds students that poor time management is the most common cause of stress. As a follow-up ask students to add four more 'time-wasters' to this list for discussion: *constant interruptions, indecision, failure to prioritise, personal disorganisation, flitting from task to task, plunging in without planning.* Remind them that they have only 168 hours in each week and ask them to think about strategies that might improve their use of time. (This is called *'reframing'* and involves finding another framework that fits the situation more effectively.)

Exams and stress is concerned with alleviating exam stress. A very useful extension activity concerns assertiveness training in relation to self-management in exam situations. Assertive statements distinguish fact from opinion and are brief and concise positive 'inner dialogues', for example *'I will....'*, *'I can'*, *'I am going to'*. Ask students to write down three things that stress them in the exams, either from previous experiences or from anticipation. Examples might be *'I never finish on time', I worry because everyone seems to write more than I do', 'I seem to write a lot but never answer the question'*. These sorts of comments represent 'faulty inner dialogues'. Next ask students to change their three comments to 'positive inner dialogues'. For example, *'I will practise and plan so that I finish the exam in good time'*. Finally, discuss how they can make their 'positive inner dialogue' come true.

RECOGNISING AND DEALING WITH STRESS

Can't cope with the stresses of studying?
Yes you can ....

By having some strategies for de-stressing you can become much more positive in your approach to studying.

What do you find stressful in your studies?

Perhaps it's the thought of an examination? Or the pressure of getting assignments in on time? Maybe it's the thought of giving a presentation?

Think of all the aspects of your studies that shout 'STRESS' to you.

[   ]

Now put a ring around one source of study-related stress that you *regularly* experience, for example, *managing time*.

OK, let's take a minute here to look at some of your reactions to that stress. That is, how did you *know* you were stressed?

Ring round your particular reactions to stress.

Drink more tea or coffee?	Not want to get out of bed?
Become emotional?	Find it difficult to sleep?
Come out in spots?	Feel shaky inside?
Have a headache?	Feel breathless?
Feel depressed?	Can't concentrate?

Add some more if you can.

[ ]

Study related stress is created by making demands on yourself. You feel these demands are difficult to off-load as someone else's problem. This means they make you feel alone and isolated and that it's all your fault and has to be dealt with by you and you alone. This is not so – there are ways to share these problems.

However, a great deal will depend upon whether you are a CALM or a CHAOS person.

The CALM approach to stress is to:

Confront the problem positively.

Approach it as something that can and has to be dealt with.

Look for the steps that need to be taken in order to deal with it.

Manage it by planning de-stress strategies.

However, the CHAOS approach is the one we often resort to. It is the CHAOS approach that leads to those stress-related reactions we saw earlier. This approach tends to:

Compromise by dealing with part of the problem but not all of it then

Hedge the problem by putting it to one side and therefore avoid commitment until we

Abandon it altogether which leads us to

Opt out of studying in general and eventually

Sink in the knowledge that we have allowed the source of the stress to become our master instead of our slave.

Let's look again at the CALM approach.

Write here, next to C, a source of stress that you have encountered in your studies - you may wish to select one from the list you made earlier.

C _____

Now, by doing that you have already **Confronted** the fact that there is a problem - and remember - problems can usually be solved.

Next, let's look at how you can **Approach** the problem – write three things here that would make the problem less stressful. (For example, you might think about *'being given more time'*, *'getting more organised'* or *'going over a piece of work on a one to one basis.'*)

A

1. _____
2. _____
3. _____

L

Look again at the approaches above and write them again here, this time in order of priority.

1. _____
2. _____
3. _____

Finally, write here how you will:

Manage these stages – how can they be achieved? Perhaps you will *'negotiate extra time with a tutor'* or *'photocopy some missed notes'*.

I will :

1. _____
2. _____
3. _____

Great, you are now well on the way to becoming de-stressed.

By finding the source of stress you are recognising that there is a problem and problems *can* be solved.

STRESS AND TIME MANAGEMENT

Do you want to know the most common cause of stress?

No, it's not having too little money for new CDs; it's having too much to do in too little time.

If only we were like the American Hopi Indians who don't even have a word for time - they have only past, present and future tense words.

However we *do* have a word for time and problems with organising time – time management – are a common cause of stress and often produce some very negative consequences.

To start with, tick which of these potential constraints on effective time management apply to you.

> I tackle things in order of which I like best.
> I do interesting things before things I am not so interested in.
> I wait until a deadline is near before I get going.
> I start with small tasks first.
> I think about the consequences of not doing a task.
> I work on tasks that involve a group first.
> I separate the urgent from the important.
> I do easy things first.
> I do the things that don't need preparations (such as research) first.
> I do the things that have the resources easily available first.
> I respond to the demands of others rather than to demands from myself.

OK, now look at the statements you ticked and put a ring round those that you know, from experience, just don't work.

Good - we've made a start because effective time and stress management depends on self-awareness.

Now, write the name of one of your subjects here. _____

Imagine that *you* are the tutor of that subject.
Write here three effective study rules related to managing time that the tutor would be likely to give you, for example – *'plan ahead'*.

1. _____
2. _____
3. _____

Compare and discuss these study rules with a fellow student.

Can you see how most time management 'rules' are basic to, not just every subject, but to life itself?

EXAMS AND STRESS

Stress is not just negative – it only becomes negative when we have more or less stress than we want. In life we constantly react to stress. Often it is the speed of the reaction that saves a life or wins a race. The stress only becomes negative when it lasts too long or becomes too strong. In order to manage stress you need to be aware of your own personal stress levels.

Examinations are common sources of stress but the stress they cause can have positive as well as negative effects.

Tick which of these positive responses affect you within an examination situation.

Increased alertness	
Quick flow of thought	
Speedy reactions	
Focused concentration	
Others? _	

Now, write three possible negative reactions to examination stress. For example, *'I can't remember what I'm reading'*.

1. _____
2. _____
3. _____

How can you deal with these negative reactions?

Well, examination stress starts at revision time. We tend to either make no revision plans and then feel guilty or make commendable but unrealistic revision plans that only a saint could keep to.

In order to combat stress, revision plans need to be **realistic**, include **exercise** and build in **variety**.

Write down here the *time* of day when you work best when and the *ways* that you prefer to revise. For example, some people are 'early birds', some like to revise through taping or condensing notes etc. etc.

OK. Now, take a couple of minutes to write down all of the rewards you are going to build in to your revision plan. For example, *going for a swim, walking the dog, playing football*.

```
┌─────────────────────────────────────────────────────────────────────┐
│                                                                     │
│                                                                     │
│                                                                     │
│                                                                     │
│                                                                     │
└─────────────────────────────────────────────────────────────────────┘
```

Right, before you start getting stressed at the thought of revision, practise this breathing technique. It's a very easy relaxation routine that you should begin to use regularly - you can even use it in the exam room. It involves taking just five breaths.

Breath one	Breathe in deeply and out fully.
Breath two	Tense your feet muscles as you breathe in and relax them as you breathe out.
Breath three	Tense your stomach as you breathe in and relax it as you breathe out.
Breath four	Tense your hands and upper part of the body as you breathe in and relax them as you breathe out.
Breath five	Tense your jaw as you breathe in and relax it as you breathe out.

Depending upon your situation you can have your eyes open or closed.

Finally, tick which of these you regularly do to alleviate examination stress during the revision period:

1. Plan revision	
2. Build in variety to revision	
3. Build in rewards	
4. Use relaxation techniques	
5. Revise with a friend	
6. Practise time management	
7. Practise past papers	
8. Exercise	
9. Work for short, sharp, focused times	
10. Keep a sense of proportion – it might be an important exam but it's not worth risking your health over	

Anything else? Compare your strategies with a fellow student.

Section 8

PREPARING FOR EXAMS

Teachers' notes
- 8.1 Organising revision
- 8.3 Planning a revision timetable
- 8.5 Making revision cards
- 8.6 Quick revision
- 8.7 Key words in exams
- 8.9 Understanding exams
- 8.11 What sort of exam taker are you?

Teachers' notes
PREPARING FOR EXAMS

The purpose of this section is to raise students' awareness of the importance of planning and preparing for revision, the range of revision techniques available and effective exam technique.

Organising revision can be used as either a warm up or as an extension activity. Students can be asked to work in pairs in order to brainstorm as many different revision techniques as they can. They may then compare their brainstorm with that of another pair. This activity can form a very useful basis for a class comparison of known revision techniques.

Planning a revision timetable is about creating extra time in what seems an already overloaded week. As a follow-up ask students to calculate how many hours in a typical week they watch television, shop and socialise. Then ask them to add up these hours and work out what they could change to create 15 extra hours for revision each week. A useful warm up or extension activity is to ask students to think of one subject they study. Ask them to prioritise each area of the subject bearing in mind the extent of knowledge already acquired. They could do this by allocating marks out of five to each area. For example, a sociology student may write '*deviance 1/5, stratification 5/5, religion 3/5.*' S/he would then know to allocate more time to *deviance* than to *stratification* on their revision timetable.

Making revision cards and **Quick revision** provide some suggestions for revision techniques. The first focuses on reducing material to key points and then stimulating the brain by using mnemonics to recall material. Students may like to warm up to the idea of mnemonics with the following activity. Ask them to teach someone who supposedly doesn't know the order of the days in the week through the use of a mnemonic (e.g. *Mary Turned West, Theo Followed Satan's Son; Many Traffic Wardens Think Fast Smile Slowly*). They could then transfer the idea of a mnemonic to some area of their studies and share it with the group or class. *Quick revision* shows how students can use what they already know as a basis for revision.

Key words in exams is designed to help with understanding the meaning of examiners' instructions. Too often students overlook these words, *discussing* when they should be *justifying* - giving *one* reason when they are asked for *reasons*. The *Bike* idea can be extended by using an activity where an incident is described (such as a fire alarm being deliberately activated without reason). Students are then asked to *describe* it, *evaluate* it, *justify* it and so on.

Understanding exams is a questionnaire that encourages evaluation of exam procedure and technique. To extend this activity students could choose any one of the 'false' statements, correct the incorrect answer and give two pieces of advice relevant to that statement. For example, '*exam instructions are clear, however you need to allow some quality time to read them and highlight key points.*' Another extension activity involves dividing students into groups. Ask one group to advise students who might have problems with statements 3, 7, 9, 10 and encourage them to write a page of tips that address managing time, reading instructions, being prepared and not misreading the questions. Give another group a similar task using statements 12, 13 18 and 19. Subsequent discussion often extends to other problems such as *'going blank'* and *'having problems getting started'*. Students can advise each other as to how best to cope with their individual exam related problems.

What sort of exam taker are you? This requires the student to think about their approach to starting an exam. Students can be encouraged to add to their *'I will'* list any other actions that will help them in the exam e.g. *wearing comfortable clothing, ensuring that the desk doesn't wobble.*

ORGANISING REVISION

You are often told to 'revise' but less often told *how* to! Effective revision involves using a variety of methods in order to keep your mind alert.

First of all fill this questionnaire in to start you thinking about your approach to revision.

	That's me	That's not me
In order to revise:		
1. I make a revision timetable		
2. I reduce my notes to key points		
3. I read up the night before the exam		
4. I transfer notes into diagrams		
5. I have no need to revise		
6. I tape the key points		
7. I am an active learner		
8. I use past exam papers		
9. I just don't know how to revise		
10. I set myself learning targets		
11. I read my notes over and over again		
12. I understand how to get facts into my long term memory		

Write here three methods of revision that work for you:

1. _____

2. _____

3. _____

Now write down which subjects you are studying and grade how 'revision efficient' you think you are on a scale of 1-10 (10 = top).

Subjects	Revision efficiency grade

© **CONNECT** Publications 1999

PREPARING FOR EXAMS   Section 8 – 2

Here is a list of essential items for revision.
- Tape recorder
- Highlighter
- 'Post-its'
- A3 and A4 size plain paper
- Clock
- Timetable
- Index Cards

Brainstorm in the space below all the other things that you consider necessary for effective revision. e.g. *a place to work*.

[ ]

Now, which of the above list of essential items can be used for each of the following.

	Items
Reducing notes to key points, marking essential pages for re-reading?	
Picking out key points, categorising different sections?	
Making revision cards?	
Listening to key points and complex information?	
Helping stick to time deadlines?	
Transferring linear notes and texts to colourful wall charts and posters?	
Keeping a day to day check on what has and has not been revised?	

Next, think of one subject that needs revising. Think how you could use each of the approaches and items listed above in that subject.

[ ]

Finally, why not get your kit together and get on your way to revising!

© **CONNECT** Publications 1999

PLANNING A REVISION TIMETABLE

Do you leave revision until the week before the exam?
Do you leave it until the day before?
Do you do any revision at all?

Well, read on and you will see that effective revision is possible if you *organise* and *plan* it.

Ask yourself the following questions.

- What activities have to be fitted into my week?
- What evenings do I have free?
- How much free time do I have in a school/college week?

Now, on this timetable, simply highlight times that you can 'earmark' for revision – be realistic – you know you won't give up all your free time and anyway you need to have a social life and not isolate yourself entirely.

	Early morning	Late morning	Early afternoon	Late afternoon	Evening
Monday					
Tuesday					
Wednesday					
Thursday					
Friday					
Saturday					
Sunday					

Right, you have made a start, now write the word 'revision' over each highlighted area – this is your framework for exam preparation – you have made a commitment.

Next, count up the highlighted revision sessions per week. _ _ _ _ _ _ _ _ _ _ _ _ _ _ _ _ _

Now count up how many weeks it is to your first exam. _

How many hours have you committed up until the examination? _ _ _ _ _ _ _ _ _ _ _ _ _

Now think about how that time should be shared out between subjects. Fill this in:

Subject	Hours per week

Subject	Hours per week

Evaluate the distribution – does it allow enough time for revision?

Remember some of your subjects will require more revision time than others.

Let's take a closer look at this. Break down each subject into topics for revision.

Subject	Topics
e.g. sociology	e.g. stratification, religion, education

Now work out how you will distribute the hours by writing on the timetable exactly what topic you will be revising and when you will be revising it. This might mean changing your previous time allocation.

Fill this in to show how many hours of revision you are now planning for each subject.

Subject	Hours

Finally, brainstorm all of the things that you have to *do* and *get* before you start revising.

For example: *highlighters, index cards to make notes, photocopies of work missed.*

How much time will you need for this essential 'getting the act together' stage?

Allow yourself quality time for this stage – it is important.

MAKING REVISION CARDS

It's important to allow our memory to have lots of positive revision boosts before an exam rather than just one long overtaxing of the poor old brain. It helps to break a subject down into 'bite size' pieces that make it less frightening and easier to learn. Try putting each 'chunk' of information onto a card.

Read the following extract.

It is generally accepted that the acidic gas sulphur dioxide is one of the principal causes of acid deposition which has damaged many lakes in Sweden and Norway. Much of this sulphur dioxide is produced from the combustion of sulphur-containing impurities when coal and oil are burned, and the pollution is transported to Scandinavia from the UK by the prevailing SW to NE air movements. Some sulphur dioxide is deposited in a dry form, the remainder dissolves in water droplets in the air to form an acidic solution of low pH, and is then deposited as 'acid rain'.

Write *sulphur dioxide* on the left hand (or front) of the 'revision card' below. Write the important information about sulphur dioxide on the right hand (or back) of the card.

Front	Back

This involves reducing the notes to key points, helping you revise as your brain has a sense of purpose.

Finally, count the main points. Think of a way of triggering these off in your memory by devising a memory booster.

Here are some examples of memory boosters:

My Very Easy Method Naming Planets (Mercury Venus Earth Mars Neptune Pluto).

StalaCtites Come from the Ceiling / StalaGmites Grow on the Ground.

Now think how you could make revision cards for each of the subjects you study.

Perhaps you could put a definition on the front and examples on the back or positive points on one side and criticisms on the other.

Finally, go and buy a pack of index cards and start revising. Don't forget that the actual act of simply making the card is a very significant part of the revision process.

PREPARING FOR EXAMS   Section 8 – 6

QUICK REVISION

One of the reassuring aspects of revision is that you will already know some of the material from your courses. This activity helps you find out what you do know already.

Look at this quick revision sheet started by one student.
The student has written what s/he already knows *before referring to any notes*. (OK, they didn't know very much.) Next they will look at any notes they have on the topic and add missing information using another colour.

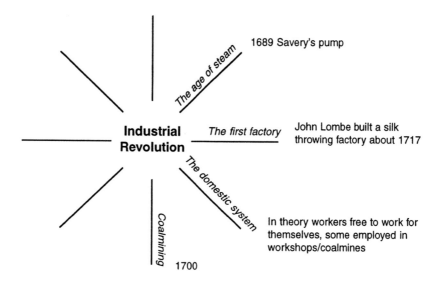

You will now need some large (A3), plain paper and some coloured pens. Using this extract from some of the student's notes, add any missing key points to the diagram above.

> **The Industrial Revolution**
> The major changes were brought about by the domestic system, the first factory, water power, the development of the steam engine, the coal mining industry, the iron and steel industry, the pottery industry, the Lancashire cotton industry, the West Riding woollen industry and the engineering industry.
> The first factory, Lombe's silk throwing mill, was powered by water. The first textile industry to become industrialised along modern lines was the Lancashire cotton industry where there was already a workforce skilled in weaving and spinning.
> The Staffordshire pottery industry thrived due to Wedgwood who made Stoke on Trent, Tunstall, Fenton, Longston, Bulslem and Hanley famous.
> Darby discovered that a strong blast of air could raise the temperature of the coke-fired furnace high enough to melt large quantities of iron ore.

By using different coloured pens you can compare how much they knew with how much they didn't know. If they were to repeat this activity on a new sheet of paper the following week, they could compare how much new knowledge they now have - a great way to revise.

Now, use this idea to check how much *you* know of any topic. Write the name of the topic in the middle of a piece of paper and construct a spider diagram as above.

You can continue checking how your knowledge is growing by repeating this activity regularly.

KEY WORDS IN EXAMS

- Do you read exam questions with care?
- Do you give quality time to thinking about what the question requires you to do?
- Have you ever written an answer and found out later that it didn't answer the question? Yes?

Well, read on and it need never happen again..

One tip that will help ensure you read the instructions is to take a **highlighter** into the exams so you can emphasise key words.

From the list of words below, put a ring round 12 key examiners' directions.

describe	reading	compare and contrast	discuss	explain
examine	the	critically evaluate	examination	justify
instructions	outline	with	summarise	care
evaluate	is	account for	to what extent	vital

Write the eight words you have not highlighted in order - reading across the page.

Now, see how quickly you can match the examiner's instruction words below to the correct definition:

Justify, Examine, Summarise, Compare, Criticise, Discuss, Contrast, Prove, Describe, Evaluate

The first has been done for you.

Explain the difference between	Contrast
Sum up the main points	
Support (with facts and/or figures, examples, references)	
Explain the similarities and differences	
Debate the issue from different viewpoints	
Give a concise statement of meaning and/or identify the main characteristics	
Identify problems/disadvantages	
Investigate closely, ask questions of	
Demonstrate, make certain	
Weigh up the strengths and weaknesses	

OK, finally we are going to put some key words into practice using the *Bike* activity. Here are two bikes.

Now...

Examine the bikes and **describe** their purpose. **Compare** the two bikes and then **explain** how they **contrast**. **Justify** the need for a bike, **comment** on the appearances of the bikes and **discuss** the effectiveness of each. **Evaluate** the usefulness of the two bikes.

Thinking of the *Bike* activity will help you to remember key words in the exam.

Finally, look through some past exam papers and find three more key words or phrases.

Write them here.

Apply them to the *Bike* activity.

UNDERSTANDING EXAMS

Test your understanding of exam procedure and technique. Decide which of these statements is true and which false.

	True	False
1. Exams are designed to catch you out.		
2. Some papers are divided into two or three parts.		
3. Exams never allow you enough time to finish.		
4. Exam instructions are never clear.		
5. You can gain marks for good spelling and grammar in some exams.		
6. Some questions in some exams are compulsory.		
7. All questions in all exams are compulsory.		
8. It is always important to arrive in plenty of time for the exam.		
9. It is always possible to borrow pens/pencils/highlighters if you've forgotten them.		
10. The exam marker makes allowances if you've misread the question.		
11. All candidates are exhausted through worry by the time the exam day arrives.		
12. It is not possible to revise for exams as you can't tell what questions will be asked.		
13. You don't know if you can take texts into the exam or not.		
14. Some questions can carry more marks than others.		
15. It is not possible to work out how much time to allow for each question.		
16. You cannot cross things out in an exam.		
17. It doesn't matter if your handwriting is illegible.		
18. You are allowed to highlight and underline on exam papers.		
19. Time spent on planning answers means you don't have enough time for a good answer.		
20. It is important to check the date of the exam as well as the starting time.		

PREPARING FOR EXAMS   Section 8 – 10

Highlight numbers 1, 3, 4, 7, 9, 10, 11, 12, 13, 15, 16, 17, 19.

These are all false. How many of them did you tick?

1 - 5   Help! You don't understand the exam system at all - take a step back, then start again by finding out what exams are all about.

6 - 8:   OK, you understand most of the exam system but maybe you don't pay enough attention to details. You might turn up at the right time on the wrong day, so beware.

10 - 12   Great, nearly top of the class! However don't be too smug - the only score should be ...

13   Yes! Your understanding of exam technique is excellent. Put your knowledge and understanding into practice and you should be an excellent exam taker.

Finally, the exams are over!!

Ring round which of these reactions you're most likely to have.

I compare answers with others	I go home and relax
I scream 'I failed'	I live in dread until the results
I predict doom and gloom	I get on with life
I accept it's over and no more can be done	I learn from the experience

Which do you think are the most helpful reactions?

© CONNECT Publications 1999

WHAT SORT OF EXAM TAKER ARE YOU?

Think back to exams or tests you've taken in the past. Did you come out thinking, *'if only I had....'*?

Write here three *'If only'* statements. For example, *'If only I had read the question more carefully'*.

1. *If only* _____
2. *If only* _____
3. *If only* _____

Now, pretend you are advising a fellow student how best to succeed in exams. Write two tips under each of the following headings:

Before the exam. In the exam. Timing answers. Answering the question. Keeping the examiner happy.

Compare your tips with a partner's if you can. If you put your suggestions together you should have a useful list of successful exam strategies.

Now the exam is about to start. The invigilator says, *'You may begin'*. Which of these should you do and which should you *not* do? Mark good advice with a tick and bad advice with a cross.

	✓ or x
a. Start writing as soon as possible	
b. Read the examiner's instructions	
c. Quickly find a question you know you can do	
d. Read through each question carefully	
e. Plan an order in which to answer the questions	
f. Look round to see who has started writing	
g. Write a time down by which you should finish each selected answer	
h. Write an outline plan for selected questions	
i. Write down the information you have learnt and will get in somewhere regardless of the question	
j. Highlight key words and analyse exactly what is required of you	
k. Show how courageous you are and seek out the most difficult question.	

Finally, write three more *'should do's'* and three more *'shouldn't do's'*.

1. _____   1. _____
2. _____   2. _____
3. _____   3. _____

(Incidentally, I hope you ticked b, d, e, g, h and j from the list above.)